Text copyright © 2008 Ruth Rothermel
Photos copyright © Ruth Rothermel

All rights reserved.

Wading River Books
PO Box 955
Wading River, NY 11792
www.wrbooks.com

WadingRiver
B O O K S

Institutional discounts available for bulk sales. Please contact us at buydirect@wrbooks.com

No part of this publication may be reproduced in whole or in part, or stored in any type of retrieval or media system, or transmitted in any form or by any means, electronic, mechanical, photocopying, or otherwise, without receiving written permission from the publisher. For specific permission please e-mail: legal@wrbooks.com

Printed in the U.S.A
1st Edition
ISBN: 978-0-9791463-1-2

Cover design and layout by Max Hergenrother

The Songs of Wildfields

By Ruth A. Rothermel

1. Merrit Hawkins homestead, built 1802. Below is a small shed. Below the shed was the "Carriage House".
2. Wildfields, built 1928.
3. Storybook Lane, built 1967.
4. Nassakeag Elementary School, built 1963.
5. Pond Path.

6. Merrit Hawkins homestead "Old House".
7. Wildfields.
8. Storybook Lane.
9. Pond Path.

Wildfields

Gently waving tall grass,
Goldenrod and daisies.
Thorny locust trees and rioting rambles.
Wildfields.
Clumps of gray bayberry and rusty cedars.
Mingling their dark branches
With the bright leaves of the pelser birch:
Crows calling harshly from the woods;
Brilliant orioles answering from the thickets:
A gray, weatherbeaten homestead nestling
Among lilac bushes and fruit trees
And facing a neat white-shingled house
across the county road –
Home of my childhood.
Home that I love!

Muriel Burnell Pettit
(Written when in high school.)

There is a crescent moon over the "Old House" and Wildfields. I look out, feeling a longing beyond belief for all that was. The lights are on at Wildfields tonight. I can place each so-familiar room. The light from what was Muriel's and my room breaks into the upstairs hall. In the kitchen below, the Tiffany-like lamp over the dining area casts a warm glow that spills beyond its boundary. Unfamiliar silhouettes move restlessly within the rooms like illegal intruders in my soul. I can barely look, but it is so compelling! "Come to me," it sings. "Come to the Wildfields that you know."

I turn away from my kitchen window to the warmth of my own home built in 1967. Three houses stand in a direct line from east to west on property my family has owned and occupied for eight generations. Fourteen generations have lived in America, beginning with Robert and Mary Hawkins who left London, England in April of 1635, sailing on a ship christened the Elizabeth and Ann. According to the Hawkins genealogy, by early summer they had built both a house and a windmill in Charlestown, Massachusetts. They had three sons and perhaps some daughters, but records were not kept of the female lines. We are descended from their son Zachariah, born in 1639. At some point in time, he came to Ashford, Long Island, which is what Setauket was called then. The earliest reference to him is in the records of the Town of Brookhaven, Long Island, under the date December 8, 1663, when he was a juror. His house was opposite the intersection of Christian and Bay avenues and has long since been torn down. Zachariah bought land from Ensign Alexander Bryan of Milford, Connecticut. In 1664 eastern Long Island was still a part of Connecticut. In 1668 he owned three of the 44 proprietary rights of the Town of Brookhaven. In 1675, on a Brookhaven valuation list filed in Albany, New York, he is listed as one of the 31 heads of families in the Town of Brookhaven. Besides his 3/44 ownership, he also had 24 acres of land and meadows by 1683. He married a Mary Biggs – possibly a second marriage, and at his death in 1699 he left eight children. Their fourth child was Eleazer, who married Sarah Owens sometime around 1711 and lived in Stony Brook, Long Island. Eleazer was both a farmer and a sea captain. On one of his voyages he came across an abandoned ship which he and his crew boarded to see what could be salvaged. Lucky Eleazer! He and his men found a large chest filled with gold and treasures. Eleazer divided it with his crew and had enough left over for him to return home and buy farms for each of his sons. One such property was the Hawkins-Mount homestead where William Sydney Mount created his farmers' paintings, located on the corner of Route 25A and Stony Brook Road in Stony Brook. Mount's paintings hang in the Museums at Stony Brook and in the Metropolitan Museum of Art in New York City.

Eleazer and Sarah had eleven children. Their second son, Alexander, married a Tabitha Satterly and they lived on a farm at Nassakeag. He was a soldier in the American Revolution and is buried in the little Hawkins Cemetery on Pond Path. He died in 1767 leaving Tabitha with six children. Their third son was Simeon, born in 1744, and who married Elizabeth (the daughter of Eleazer's son, David). Confused? I'll make a chart! You see there wasn't much to pick from in those 31 families out here in the wilds of Brookhaven, except for some other inbred families as crazy as they were. And besides, who wanted to date some girl a half a day's ride on horseback away?

But I have a real affinity for Simeon because I've been in his house, touched the wooden pegs and beams, climbed his staircase and sat under the same big oaks to play with my dolls. By that time, Simeon's house was "the Carriage House" and was also Grandpa's garage. I'd have gone down into Simeon and Elizabeth's cellar – a small dugout area facing Pond Path – but the snakes down there scared me. Dad used the remaining upstairs room for his workshop where he put together bookcases of metal scraps while amusing me with his singing. I followed him everywhere, even when I was nineteen and he was dying. And when I was a little girl, I sat on his bench in "Simeon's house" and cut out paper dolls using the models' pictures in the Sears Roebuck catalogue.

Simeon farmed the land around his home in Nassakeag and raised six children there, including two sets of twins: Joel and Nathan, who never married, and Tabitha and Mary, who did. Mary married a Zopher Hawkins (yes, another Hawkins) who, during the War of 1812, used his team to haul a cannon to Stony Brook to drive off a British warship in Stony Brook Harbor.

After three daughters were born, Simeon and Elizabeth had a son who they named Merritt, born Nov. 6, 1777. When Merritt talked of marrying Anna Hawkins (yes, another Hawkins!), Simeon helped his son build a home nearby, the family homestead where we lived until 1928, the "Old House."

Merritt farmed the land at Nassakeag until his death in 1849. Elizabeth had died 27 years earlier. Both are buried, as are his parents, in the Hawkins Cemetery on Pond Path. They had eight children, the eldest of whom, David, drowned in the Mississippi River in 1855. The fifth child, daughter Sarah Ann, born in 1815, was my great-great grandmother and she married Ebenezer (you guessed it) Hawkins. One of their other children, Bryant Coleman, born in 1819, was a piano manufacturer in a factory on the hill across from the Methodist Church about where the *Three Village Herald* is published in East Setauket. And I know every inch of Merritt's home.

I went upstairs in the Merritt Hawkins homestead but rarely, but I lived in that house for the first five years of my life. Nana and Grandpa Selleck slept downstairs in the small "borning room" off the living room. Mama, Daddy, Muriel and I slept in the big bedroom which had once been the kitchen until a new kitchen room was built on the north side. Our room had a fireplace with an oven, its windows facing the south and east. Daddy built cradles for Muriel and me when we were newborns; we slept in them until we were old enough for cribs. Mama and Daddy slept in their large bed between our cradles and cribs. The headboard leaned against the east wall. The path from the kitchen door went past our bedroom, past the syringa bush where we slept in our baby carriages, out to Pond Path (which may have been called Ackerly's Path then). Many photos show the syringa brush now cut down by tenants. Grandpa's father, Ethelbert Selleck, often sat near the bush with one of us by his knee.

Merritt Hawkins married the eldest child of William Hawkins; Anna was the first bride to live in the "Old House." She died while her children were still young. Decator, her youngest, was only two. Her son, Elkanah, was a blacksmith in Stony Brook. Their daughter, Amanda Maria, married Louis Selleck of Middletown, New York. So many Brookhaven families were drawn to the fertile Hudson Valley and Orange County area that we are forever finding strands of the family web connecting there.

My daughter Carol and her descendants are also related to William Hawkins through her father, William Nelson Ackerly. William's son George was his second child and can be traced to Carol through six generations.

William's younger daughter Ruth (18 years younger than Merritt's wife, Anna), was only four when her father died. Her older sister Anna raised her in the "Old House." As she grew up, Ruth undoubtedly helped raise Sarah Ann, Anna's daughter. How often did they sit before the great fireplace that occupied most of the eastern wall of the living room? How often did they take the Bible from the corner cabinets? If they came in the south-facing front door, they would have entered the angled foyer, one door opening into the kitchen, the other into the living room. The dining room was on the northern side and from it a narrow staircase turned sharply and led upward to the rooms above. A door also opened to the cellar stairs where the canned goods and herbs were kept in the damp dark room below. My memories of the cellar are of walking into a large spider web on the stairway and finding dozens of tiny spiders all over me. I can't remember ever going into that cellar again.

When Merle was about six, she and her mother and father came to live with us because her mother, Aunt Ardie, was so ill with tuberculosis. Because she was so sick, Muriel and I were not allowed upstairs, but Merle came down to play with us. Years later, Mom took me up there one day and showed me each room and told me who had slept in it. These memories of the years I lived there float through my brain. Grandpa sat in a large chair – the Morris Chair – on the south side of the living room as he read his daily paper. One day Merle, Muriel and I were playing in our bedroom. Merle suggested we get some action going by slamming the bedroom door. We did so three or four times with Grandpa calling out, "Stop that!" as we giggled hysterically after each BAM! Suddenly, Grandpa materialized before us. He never said a word. It was quiet enough to hear the clouds moving in the heavens above us. He went back to his chair and I wet my pants.

Great grandpa Ethelbert Selleck grew up in Middletown, New York. He and his wife, Hester Ann Hawkins, daughter of Merritt and Sarah Ann, lived there until our grandpa, Ethelbert Hawkins Selleck, was seventeen. They owned a dry-goods store which burned down. When Sarah Ann became ill, Hester Ann and Ethelbert returned to the "Old House" to care for her. Ethelbert's sister wrote to him often. Before he married Hester Ann, Ethelbert often wrote from his rooming place in New York City to his bride-to-be on Long Island. He worked for E.S. Mills and Co. in their store on White Street. In one such letter, he wrote on August 28, 1864: "Dearest Het, You must not give yourself so much uneasiness concerning the draft. I don't really think that there will be a draft in the city. If we get the credit for the troops that have been furnished to the Navy Department our quota is full, I don't give myself any uneasiness and I shall wait the decision of the Provost Marshall before I get alarmed. I won't go even should I be drafted, if it has to take every cent of money that I ever had – so rest assured that Eth will not leave his darling to fight for "Uncle Abe."

Hester Ann and Ethelbert were married in 1864. In 1879 Hester Ann's mother Sarah Ann died, followed closely by her grieving father – who took his own life within the walls of the "Old House." Merle's mother, Ardell, was just the last of many who died there. Grandpa was building Wildfields, hoping to move Ardell to the sunporch to give her air and sunlight. He hoped these would restore his daughter-in-law to health, but she died earlier that summer of 1928 while we were all still living in the "Old House." Ardell was a lovely brown-eyed woman, sweet and gentle. My father lifted me up to see her in her casket in the living room. "She's an angel now," he said. At the age of four, I believed that to be exactly what an angel looked like.

We moved into Wildfields that December; into the beautiful home that Grandpa had built for Elsie our Nana, and which they shared so unselfishly with many of us.

On page 65 of <u>Port Jefferson, Story of a Village</u>, it is stated that Mather Hospital had only been founded the year before Ardell died, and really didn't open until 1929. Before that time, all were cared for by local country doctors or by their families. Hester Ann and Ethelbert Selleck, Grandpa's parents, died in the "Old House," as did Sarah Ann and Ebenezer. All are buried in the Hawkins Cemetery still located beside Pond Path, Setauket, Long Island, New York. It wasn't until Ardell's death that family members were buried in the cemetery of the North Congregational Church in Mt. Sinai, New York and later in the Presbyterian churchyard in Setauket and at Cedar Hill Cemetery in Port Jefferson, New York. It is the latter where my husband, Victor, is buried and where I will someday rest.

The little cemetery on Pond Path was the one for the South Setauket Free Christian Church, located on Bennett's Road on the property now owned by James Wilson. The first records were made in 1884 when Elbert W. Hawkins, Ethelbert Selleck and George W. Smith were the trustees. Rev. W.H. Little was the minister.

In 1894, Hester Ann Selleck was the treasurer of the Ladies Aid Society and reported $235.32 on hand (something like my bank account!) which was placed in the Riverhead Savings Bank. Ten dollars of the money came from renting out a large church-owned tent for fairs and activities in other nearby congregations. In 1897, the pastor received a salary of $2.00.

By 1926, the church was closed. Grandpa, Ethelbert H. Selleck became the chairman of the South Setauket Cemetery Association. In a meeting he called on August 11, 1926, Alida Holgerson (Alice Selleck's grandmother) was elected president of the association. Grandpa, E.H. Selleck, Ethel Selleck Pettit (my mother) and Melanthan Hawkins were made trustees. The cemetery was kept clean; fences built and repaired. For years, Floyd Holgerson cleaned and trimmed faithfully the cemetery for $4.00 each spring before Memorial Day, and again in the fall.

By 1950, there was a revived cemetery organization whose members paid $1 a year in dues for the upkeep of the cemetery. In 1973, my husband, Victor Rothermel, and I joined the association and remained members until the cemetery was turned over to the Hawkins Association in 1979.

Recently, permanent plaques have been placed on the graves of Alexander and Zopher Hawkins who were soldiers in the Revolutionary War. It's a quarter of a mile to the cemetery from the "Old House" and from Wildfields.

Ardell's death brought about profound changes in the household where we lived. Ardell's immediate family was not close by. She was the daughter of Col. Charles Whittlesey from the Boston area. Ardell had one sister, Leslie, who married a man named O'Done and they were divorced with two children. Ardell and Bernard had but one daughter, Merle Elizabeth. Merle often visited her Aunt Leslie in Plainview, New Jersey, during summer vacations. She also established a lasting relationship with Jessie Nairn who lived nearby. Ardell had an Aunt Elizabeth Whittlesey who visited with us at Wildfields every year for months at a time. We all loved "Auntie" dearly. She always took Merle on an excursion to New York City to go shopping and then to buy "butter cakes" at Child's Restaurant.

When Hester Ann's parents were gone, the Nassakeag farm was idle. As Hester Ann was an only child, she inherited all of the property. In 1881 Ethelbert and Hester Ann gave up their Middletown, N.Y. home and moved to Setauket to the "Old House." Hester Ann kept a diary of the first two years of their life there. On November 15, 1883 she wrote:

"15th – Digging out firewood along the fences and fixing fences. Shook and gathered in the rock apples."

"17th – Bertie sorting corn. Eth cutting up hedge row south of new lot. Knitting Eth's mittens. Done house cleaning a week ago, all but kitchen.

"March 24th/84 – Bertie found his first duck egg."

"April 1st/84 – Town meeting today. Eth and Bertie started about 12 o'clock for Coram."

"April 15/84 – Eth commenced plowing for more oats and went to New York after fertilizer."

"April 23/84 – Mary, Auntie and I cut three bushels of potatoes for Bertie and Mr. Robinson to plant. Eth is getting his oats ground ready. Mary and I cleared out the "Old House" (Simeon's home) ready to get the church quilt on. Burnt our meat."

"May 3rd/84 – I cleaned the lower bedroom. Bertie's black hen came off with 10 chicks. Eth bought of B. Edwards 4,000 strawberry plants for $1.50 per thousand."

"May 6/84 – Eth plowed up field and Auntie and I set out strawberry plants."

"May 20/84 – Whitewashed, cleaned and got carpet nearly down in my room."

"Oct 2/84 – Eth and I went to Riverhead Fair."

"Nov 20/84 – Eth bought two turkeys – .15 cents lb."

"Nov 26/84 – Stuffed and cooked the turkeys. In the afternoon Mary made 51 crullers and in the eve we mixed bread and biscuits before going to Silves W."

"Nov 27/84 – Thanksgiving – Baked bread and biscuits and set table for eve. 51 took tea."

I close my eyes and see Wildfields turning backward in time and I can hear and see and smell the scenes, for they are still here for me or in my memories. The buildings, fences, and fields were all there for me. Only the forms and faces have gone. I wish those strawberry fields were still here! The fields and lawns between the houses held sheep and cows and horses; they have been fields of flax, vegetables and flowers; they have been fields of produce grown by farmers who'd rented the land . The clotheslines still stand behind Wildfields where sheets and towels smashed at the leaves and grasses in a Long Island breeze. In the spring we hung the rugs over those lines, wearing dust caps on our heads, and beat them with the bamboo and wire carpet beaters. The dust flew into our eyes and mouths, choking us. In the summer we weeded long rows of beets, beans, cucumbers, carrots, Swiss chard, corn and tomatoes – and Mama's flowers – in Ethelbert's garden. It was the same sweet earth that Simeon and Merritt and Ebenezer and Ethelbert farmed, and farmed by the generations that followed, and will be farmed by those to come.

Some thirty-two years after Ethelbert Selleck wrote of the Civil War draft, their only child, Ethelbert Hawkins Selleck, had married my grandmother, Elsie E. Burnell. In a letter she wrote to her mother-in-law Hester Ann, who was living on the Nassakeag farm, Elsie penned, "Your letter came with my Christmas present enclosed. Please accept many thanks for the same. I'd like to clap it in the bank, but Bert thinks I'd better clap it on my back.

"I got such a dreadful cold wearing my cape out one cold day after Christmas. So now I stay in the house until I can get a cloak to wear.

My cold is better, but my lung feels sore yet. I cough some yet, and my nose is half as big again as ordinary from blowing it so much."

Nana must have been a sight! She was not noted for having a small nose to begin with!

By 1897 Ethelbert H. and Elsie were living in Newark, N.J. and raising my mother, Ethel, and my uncle, Bernard. Mom spent part of her summers in Nassakeag and part with her mother's sister, Aurelia Gray, who lived on 25A in Setauket, not far from Woods Corner.

On January 21, 1905 Hester Ann Selleck died, leaving Ethelbert alone on the Nassakeag farm. Ethelbert H., their only child, felt it a duty to return to Setauket to be with his aging father, so Grandpa and Nana moved into the "Old House." Grandpa knew farm life well. His boyhood diary from life on the Nassakeag farm was much as I remember him. Grandpa had very little to say. Some excerpts from his diary, written in 1882 read thus:

    Wednesday, January 11th – School
    Saturday, January 14th – Wrote to Grandma
    Tuesday, January 17th – Papa came home.
    Saturday, January 21st, Sunday January 22, Monday January 23, Tuesday January 24 – Chicken pox.
    Saturday April 15th – Set purple 13 eggs. Harrow oak lot. Spaded my garden.
    Sunday May 14 – Didn't go anywhere
    Tuesday May 23 – Squashed ten caterpillars. Cart hay into barn.
    Sunday July 9 – Sunday School and church. Mr. Allen – New Village – preached
    Saturday August 12th – Went to Port Jefferson. Went to circus.
    Monday – Thrashed oats.
    Wednesday, August 30 – Went to Port Jefferson. Manure.
    Wednesday, September 13 – Went to asylum (not stay).
    Wednesday, October 25 – Cut up wood. Went to mill. Went to Stony Brook.
    Monday, December 25 – Our Christmas tree best of all.
    Sunday, December 31 – South Setauket Sunday School and church Goodbye 1882 Ditto Diary

Within seven years of writing his diary, Ethelbert had met Elsie Burnell, daughter of Dr. Sereno Burnell of Wading River, Long Island. Sereno's wife Ruth Burghardt bore him four daughters and a son who died in infancy. Ruth Susanna Burghardt was born in London, England, when her parents returned there from America on a business trip. Her father, George Burghardt, was a fur trader. Her mother, Eliza Troll Burghardt, had also been born in London but settled on Long Island with George. She is buried in Patchogue. She had seven children before she died at age 47.

Ethelbert H. and Elsie were married in October of 1889. Dr. Burnell, (whose father was also named Sereno and also a doctor) was a typical country doctor. He moved finally to Setauket in a house across from the Thompson House on Main Street, next to what is now Gallery North.

That house is believed to have burned down. Sereno and Ruth raised my grandmother while still living in Wading River.
When Ethelbert H. and Elsie were expecting their first child, they were living in Bayonne, New Jersey. Grandpa worked in New York City.

One story told is that Nana came to Setauket to be with her father, Sereno, at this baby's birth. When Grandpa got word that his wife had gone into labor, he took the first train going east on the Long Island Railroad. That train, however, only went so far and he traveled the rest of the way on foot: When he came to a trestle which had no hand rail, possibly at King's Park, he crawled across on hands and knees. He arrived tired, safe, and proud of the birth of my mother. It was July 14, 1891. Their second child, Louis Bernard, was born in Bayonne, New Jersey, on November 28, 1894. Following this birth, Nana contracted tuberculosis which she fought valiantly for years.

Sereno Burnell Sr. practiced in Miller Place, N.Y. and his son, Sereno, practiced in Wading River and Setauket. Upon his death, Dr. Burnell's practice went to Dr. Squires of Stony Brook which explains why Aunt Aurelia (nana's sister) and Nana were so close to "Auntie Squires," his wife. Their son, Dr. Duane Squires, later took over the practice and became our family doctor when we were kids. Nana and "Auntie Squires" died within two days of each other in March 1934. "Auntie Squires" had a severe stroke prior to her death. A frail, sweet woman, she would come for a day's visit even when she could no longer talk. Muriel and I would walk her through Mom's flower gardens. She re-learned how to say "yes" and "no," but that was all. We were so fond of her and it was hard to see tears in her eyes as she struggled to communicate.

Nana died of pneumonia and the complications of a long illness. She had many gastro-intestinal problems and took her phosphate soda every day, her cure for all ills. She never slept in her bed in her later years, but sat in the wooden captain's chair in the kitchen at night because of all her pain and discomfort. She said she'd never go into a hospital for surgery – and she never did. She probably died as a result. I was very close to her. I remember running from the bus every day, into the house, through the dining room, and over to where her mahogany rocker was tilted back, Grandma's feet on the living room radiator. One day she said, "You know that you may come home one day soon and find me gone." I was devastated. At eleven, I didn't think that anything could change this wonderful family cluster, but a few months later it did. A hospital bed was put in Wildfields' living room, against its east wall. At times, Nana sat in a chair picking at the air and her clothes. Family myth said this was a sign of death. The sliding doors into the dining room were closed and we children had to stay quietly on the dining room side or go up to our rooms. One night; just after supper, Uncle Nard (Bernard) came through those doors with tears in his eyes. We all looked up. "I must go and get Father from the barn," he said. Nana was gone.

Grandpa was lonely beyond belief. It was Nana who had organized our lives, set the pace, made the rules. In her kind way she left no question that things would be done her way. Grandpa complied with her every wish. As he had in the "Old House," he sat in his chair in the living room at Wildfields – in the center of the room – smoking his pipe, listening to the radio, reading his paper. He was an elder in the Setauket Presbyterian Church which he attended faithfully. He was a member of the Royal Arcanum. He played cards with Percy Smith of Stony Brook and occasionally visited old friends. Sometimes he went to Pound Ridge and stopped to drive past his old Middletown, N.Y. friendly streets, once hi home. He fed and milked his cows and chickens and tended his wonderful vegetable garden. But his heart ached for his Elsie.

Grandpa built Wildfields according to Nana's wishes. Their little bedroom was downstairs with a lavatory built next to it. She narrowed the width of the house, definitely changing the beautiful lines of a Dutch Colonial home. But we thought it was paradise.

This is where I lived, home. These are my roots, our roots, my security, my heart. The breath of generations before us lingers over the gentle fields. There was a time when the trees were so low that one could see the Long Island Sound from the juncture of Pond Path and Upper Sheep Pasture Roads, or so Uncle Nard told his son David, who told me. Trees were cut for homes and fuel and to open fields for planting, and all who lived between here and the waters of the bays farmed the land. Those at the water edge built ships and sailed to New York City with cut wood for fuel and buildings there, and others went far out to sea for whales, or stayed nearer shore to fish and dig for clams and oysters.

Grandpa worked on Wall Street in New York City and did volunteer work with Herbert Hoover in the Danish Relief Program. When he retired from these jobs, he moved to Setauket and became a "gentlemen farmer.." Bernard had married Ardell and was doing some farming there. He later moved to Main Street., Setauket, where Ardell worked as a telephone operator from their home next to the Tucker Jones house. Their daughter, Merle Elizabeth, was born on June 26, 1920. Bernard was now working in the little Setauket Post office at the edge of the Upper Mill Pond on Main Street. Uncle Nard was also forming a jazz band. He played the piano by ear and taught me six or seven basic chords when I was a teenager so that I, too, could play by ear. His band later practiced at Wildfields and many nights I fell asleep to the jazz beat below me.

The year that Merle Elizabeth was born, my mother and father were married and took up residence with Nana and Grandpa in the "Old House." It was the fall of 1920 and Grandpa had several cows and two horses, Tom and Shea. He had long, long rows of vegetables in the fields east of the house. The north field held stacks of hay and was bordered by locust fences. Some of these fences were still there in the thirties and early forties bordering Upper Sheep Pasture Road. At one time the family owned all of the land between Upper and Lower Sheep Pasture Roads, except for one small parcel. Some fields were bordered with apple trees and cherry trees. The pond bay at the end of a path going down the hill from the front of the "Old House." Halfway to the pond was a well. Its wooden structure rose some four feet above the rock base, with a wooden top upon which the bucket sat, tied with a long rope for lowering. When we lived in the homestead, there was a hand pump in the kitchen sink; under the beds were chamber pots that needed emptying in the outhouse, no matter what the weather. Kerosene lamps burned at night. The big iron stove in the kitchen burned wood and then coal. Nana would poke the metal handle into the slot of the stove lid and lift it off. Then she'd fill the little shovel, pushing it into the coal scuttle and dropping the coal into the open space on top. With the removable handle, she'd put the lid back on and the fire would glow through the openings in the side grate. The big tea kettle would begin to sing and the cups and saucers would come off the shelf in the big white cupboard.

In the early mornings, Daddy brought me from the bedroom and sat me in my highchair next to the stove while he measured coffee into a big agate pot, pumped water into it, and sat it on the big iron stove. One day he cut a grapefruit in two, slicing the sections and giving me some. I loved it. No one had ever had grapefruit to give me before. Mama came into the room and immediately scolded Dad that I was "too young" to eat grapefruit. Such amazing fears!

I also remember a more justifiable scolding. I took a knife from the kitchen to pare an apple as I'd see the grown-ups do. Soon blood was gushing from my finger. I sat on my bed weeping, trying to stop the flow. That's where Muriel and Merle found me and "tattled." Lucky that they did. It took some doing by Nana, Mama and Uncle Nard to stop the bleeding. I was sure that Mama would make me bring a branch from the bush outside. She often made us get switches which she used on our leg – I didn't even scream when they poured peroxide on my wound. I didn't dare! I'd never been yelled at like that before, and there were three big bodies to my five-year-old one. You'd have thought I'd have cut my arm off!

Every spring Grandpa would watch his "sitting hens" to see where their nests were. When the babies hatched, we were all allowed to choose one to call our own. They were all so cute. I've never figured out why something that adorable has to grow up to be a smelly chicken. Once we took one for our own; we fed it oatmeal and water and put it in a shoebox. Needless to say, our young hands had little to do with nurturing this fluffy baby and there were many tearful funerals at the gravesites near the drain from the kitchen. I surely hope that my belief is true – that the afterlife is nothing but peace and joy. Life is so wonderful, but death to those who are left here is terrible. Somehow little chicken didn't look like Ardell Angel.

Simeon's home (the "Carriage House") and Merritt's home, which now was Grandpa Ethelbert H.'s home, was soon to change again. Merritt's wife, Anna, grew up about where Smith Haven Mall now stands. For the first time since she had left her home to marry Merritt, her descendants would leave to go to a new home. Ardell was becoming increasingly sicker with tuberculosis and Grandpa decided to build a new home across the road directly east of the "Old House." It would have central heat, toilets, hot water, electricity, and a sunporch where Ardell could get well.

I heard the tap-tap-tapping of hammers and would look up from my sand pile in the walkway near the kitchen door. Mama had forbidden me to ever cross the road alone to where the new house was being built. It was "too dangerous" and I was "adventuresome." (Too much traffic? Perhaps a car every hour or so!) But I was also obedient, so I sat by myself watching the giant boards go into place, like a sketch of a house appearing line by line until the frame of our beautiful new home appeared. It was Nana's and Grandpa's house, but it would be our *home*. Muriel and Merle were in school and I would start in September. We moved into Wildfields in December of 1928.

When the stairs were built, they looked like the Bible pictures I had seen of Jacob's ladder going into the heavens. Muriel and I were not allowed upstairs in the "Old House" because Aunt Ardell was ill, so stairs would be a special thing. Most of the hay field was gone and I could see across to the woods beyond. Mama had shown me just where the clothesline would go. I could imagine my doll's clothes blowing in the breeze. And upstairs there would be a bathroom and Muriel and I would share our room. Sometimes all these things frightened me. I had never slept away from my parents' side. Mama told me that there would be a door between their room and ours. I tried to see just where that would be.

When we finally moved into Wildfields, Merle was with us. Muriel and I had twin metal beds that Daddy bought from Gaseau Tompkins, where he worked in Brooklyn. We were in the northwest front bedroom. Merle had her three-quarter metal bed in the front room next to ours. Her room opened into a large closet and on to the sun porch. Sometimes Uncle Nard slept there until he remarried and brought Aunt Margaret to live in the "Old House." Merle never was asked to live with them and she grew up with Muriel and me as sisters. Nana and Grandpa slept in the little bedroom downstairs; Mama and Daddy in the northeast bedroom above them.

Muriel and I had rose-colored spreads, satiny and soft, that were folded up every night and draped over the feet of the beds. Mama bought them at Sweezey and Newins in Patchogue, as she did so many of our things. We had a table lamp with a rose-colored shade that made a warm glow in the room. Mama's closest girlhood friend, whom we called Aunt Dell, had painted her a watercolor of roses and it hung over our beds.

Aunt Dell was a great inspiration to me later in my life. A print of the head of Christ hung over our desk. Mama put lacy curtains in the windows. Daddy made us each doll houses which were soon filled with furniture and porcelain doll families. My doll house had a flat roof, so we piled up big dolls and stuffed animals on top. Grandpa won a big brown dog at the Setauket Firemen's Carnival which he gave to us. Muriel had a red stuffed elephant with white ivory tusks. Mama had bought us matching wicker chairs and huge dolls before we left the "Old House." They wore real baby clothes, big enough for a toddler. When Muriel was in her fifties she saw the dolls in the little red barn and asked Aunt Margaret for them. She was refused. "They belong to the estate," which Aunt Margaret had inherited. They probably became pillows for raccoons living in there.

One morning recently, I sat sipping hot black coffee, looking west out of the dinette windows at 8 Storybook Lane, looking toward my beloved Wildfields. Birds swung past the feeders in my backyard. My eyes followed the path through the open gate, across the field of still-green clover and winter stubble, to the clothes poles. Six of them stood as neatly as they did the day they were put there some sixty years ago, except for some missing paint scratched off by not-so-gentle Long Island winds and rains. Their white knobs have held many birds resting from flight from the pond to the west, across the open fields and into the hedges. We had marked these hedges with spruces that coarsely bushed the sky and just as gently sheltered cardinals and chickadees alike. There trees were the offspring of the giants on the north side of the house at Wildfields; they clung to the earth and grew as "children at their mother's knee." Now they, too, reached into the heavens.

And then, the first robin appeared – red-breasted and lean from the flight north. It looked up toward the sky and God ... and sang.

The neighbor's cat slouched up the path, striped and beautiful. Seeing my face in the window, he let out a plaintive greeting. Somewhere from the "Old House" across Pond Path, the tenant's dogs barked. The cat, sensing no immediate danger, found my eyes again and wailed,

"Some more! Please, feed me." (Since that day, he has *moved* in, claiming squatter's rights. He's been named Stripuss and seldom, if ever, returns from whence he came.)

Cousin Dave Selleck's chainsaw started up beyond the little barn. It was a comfort to know that a relative was close by. David is the heartbeat of Wildfields, and although he is eight years my junior, he knows more of the history of this place than I ever will. We share many stories, many remembrances. Perhaps today he'll come in for coffee and the songs of Wildfields will go on.

When I think of David, I think first of a little boy standing in the rose arbor opening at the path to the "Old House," calling, "Roosie, come!" I'd soon be at his side, racing from Wildfields, crossing Pond Path to hug him and take him with me to play. We'd find a young locust grove in the north field and fashion a house of trodden grass. Out came my little chair and my sister's white one, and the basket of teacups, spoons, and teddy bears. Then it was so easy – being ten and drinking sunshine, with nothing intruding but love and joy. In summer the fields were filled with daisies. There were garlands to make by poking holes in the stems and then slipping another daisy through the hole until the garland reached around our waists or hung from the thorny locust branches. We seemed a hundred miles from the rest of the world. There was no traffic, no hum or noise of nearby highways, no sirens, no helicopters racing overhead as they approach the University hospital; there were just the songs of birds and bees and frogs and Grandpa's "Pet" moving in her field or stall, David laughing and Mama singing from within Wildfields.

In winter, when I look across the fields to the homes I knew, I see the ice glistening in the path – a hazard now to my aged bones. Except for its beauty on the sparkling trees, the ice frightens me. The winds will soon shatter the ice to the ground like so much broken glass. I walk gingerly to the two bird feeders, praying that these old bones won't shatter, too. Squirrels scamper by and chickadees follow me, almost landing on my hands. Blue jays swing in from the evergreens surrounding Wildfields. Tufted titmice, cardinals, sparrows, nut hatches, red-headed and downy woodpeckers, filchers, finches and juncos are all waiting for me from atop branches of evergreens where they take refuge. The path to Wildfields is littered with small branches and ice particles. The rhododendrons have closed up tight, pencil slits of leaves curled against the cold.

I can remember long ago putting on my skates and skating on the frozen front lawn at Wildfields. Every winter we waited for the pond below the "Old House" to freeze. It was a small pond with a tiny island in the middle where ducks made their nests. A large tree had fallen into the pond and was a resting place for turtles, sunning themselves, and for us it was a learning place In the spring I would crawl out upon that huge tree and scoop frog eggs from the black water below. I'd take them to school to watch them hatch into pollywogs and then turn magically into frogs. We learned to skate on the pond and did so until we were old enough to go to the mill pond which froze every winter in those days. We skated on the pond opposite the Neighborhood (Community) House because the upper north pond seldom froze solid. Two of the Setauket families lost their sons skating on that pond one winter day. One was a white boy from the Lyons family; the other a black child from the Sells family who tried to save his friend and went in with him.

One day I stayed too long at our little pond. My feet and hands began to burn and I had difficulty removing my skates and putting my shoes on. I found that I couldn't walk without great pain, so I crawled up the hill and across Pond Path toward the house. The lawn seemed endless. Nana and Mama removed two pair of sweaty socks, sat me in a dining room chair and immersed my purplish feet in tepid water until the pain subsided. This is a memory which returns vividly every winter when I'm out in the cold!

Down on the Mill Pond, old Mr. Tyler taught his neighbor's child, little Martha Wells, to do figure-eights. She was about four and he was an old man. We watched in wonder. His house still rests al the very edge of the pond nearest the Melville bridge by the post office. As our high-school years approached, there was new meaning to the ponds. Skating parties took place. Bonfires were the places where dreams were made, hot, steaming cocoa passed around in metal cups. Boys were there beside us; skating was a partnership. Hands were held, bodies stayed close and warm. No pot, no pills, no alcohol. Life was full of simple laughter and love.

In the spring, the little pond was a different place. The snakes lay along the ledges of stone in the old well. On warm sunny days we knew that they would be out there and sometimes they would be close to the top of the wells. If so, we looked gingerly over the side. If they were nearer the bottom, we dropped pebbles to see if we could stir them into action, and then ran squirming and giggling to the end of the path at the pond.

At spring's first stirring, I'd get a quart mason jar and cross the marshy places at the pond's edge. They were thick with brown leaves and dark mud, but one piece of the mossy land jutted out near the big log and there, in that dark water, I could always find clusters of frog's eggs.

In March, I could hear the peepers (tree frogs) at night from my bedroom window at Wildfields. (I still can from Storybook Lane). Leaning on my elbows on my windowsill, I'd listen to them as they sang me into dreams. Spring was here … spring … spring and walks with Daddy through the woodlot road to find pussy willows. Mama would send us three girls out to locate arbutus, and we knew just where to look. Its fragrance was never equaled in our gardens. The rare arbutus trailed close to the ground with tiny stems and green-brown leaves. We often found it hidden under leaves in the woods. Most of the flowers were white or pale pink but occasionally a deep, bright pink one would appear like a lost treasure. Each year Mama sent a box of it to an invalid lady friend who was wheelchair-bound. Like the ground pine, the arbutus is now gone forever, covered with schools and play yards and houses and streets.

One other thing has left us: the whip-poor-will. Its plaintive call reached our hearts each
evening. When we were three little girls, Nana taught us many songs. One that we especially loved went:

> "Oh meet me when daylight is fading
> And darkening into the night
> When songbirds are singing their vespers
> And the day has long vanished from sight.
> Oh, then, I will tell to you only
> The love I have cherished so long
> If you will but meet me this evening
> When you hear the first whip-poor will song.
> Whip-poor-will.
> Whip-poor-will.
> Hear the first whip-poor-will song.
> Oh meet me - Oh meet me.
> Oh meet me - Oh meet me.
> When you hear the first whip-poor-will song."

When I returned to live at Wildfields in 1967, there were whip-poor-wills still singing in the hills south of us but, as houses were built there and eradicated their peaceful domain, they disappeared. In February 1989 (I marked it in my bird book), I heard a *whip-poor-will* close by.

I went quickly to the kitchen window and the direction from which the song was coming. There on the branch of the nearest maple tree, was one of the dark brown birds. He sang one more beautiful whip-poor-will for me and disappeared over the fields in flight.

Some evenings there were owls outside in the hedges; pheasants walked through the fields; barn swallows and chimney swifts circled at dusk. They are all gone now. When we hung the clothes on the outside lines, gray kingbirds would dive-bomb us in the spring when their nests were close by.

We were forever chasing them away by swinging the clothes poles at them. The clothes poles were long pieces of wood with forked ends that were used to push the lines up when they were too heavy with wet clothes.

In the autumn, the fox hunts occurred in or near Grandpa's woods. Mr. Melville and friends organized them and all the "beautiful people" in their velvet coats and hats mounted up and chased some poor beast across south Setauket, hounds baying and leading the way. I must admit it was exciting to hear and see, but I always prayed that they'd never catch the fox.

When we moved into Wildfields that winter of 1928, there were eight of us living there, among them Nana (Elsie Burnell Selleck) who was a small, chubby lady eccentric to the last degree. She ran the house with little or no regard to schedules. She loved music, was a devout Christian who never felt well enough to go to church. She cared nothing at all for style and wore baggy cotton dresses the year round, with nothing but underpants underneath. She never wore her false teeth unless absolutely necessary and happily gummed her food, "absolutely necessary" meaning that she had to go out into the public. Then the teeth went in and a pained expression took over. She went to a barber in Port Jefferson to keep her hair cut in a very short bob. The kitchen was her domain. She washed all of the glassware and left it sitting on the corner of the sink. No one ever put it away. Every night at about eight o'clock or later, she scrubbed the linoleum kitchen floor and placed newspapers on it to dry. Then she started supper. She was the most caring person I ever knew. She laughed at difficulties. Her warm, fat body was a great nesting place.

Grandpa (Ethelbert Hawkins Selleck) was a quiet man of average height and built. He was distinguished by his quiet attitude and powerful presence. His head was bald except for a rim of white hair circling the lower portion. Unlike Nana, he kept a rigid routine of feeding chickens after his breakfast of one three-minute egg with toast and coffee, going to the barn to care for his cows and horses, going for the evening mail and paper, feeding the chickens again, napping in the big overstuffed chair in the living room (which Mom bought to replace the Morris chair), eating his cornflakes with milk before going to bed. He opened his heart and his home to all of us and quietly watched us grow. He never missed a Sunday at church unless he was ill or away, sitting in his assigned pew on the left side facing the altar.

Grandpa's daughter (Ethel Burnell Selleck Pettit), my mother, was a tiny nervous woman of four feet eleven inches in height. She loved everyone, seldom got angry, seldom made decisions on her own, was a fanatically devout Christian who also never missed church if she could help it; she saw to it that we three girls attended Sunday School and church throughout the year and Bible school in the summer. She had a fear of cancer (which to our knowledge she never had) and a fear of dying in general, as she didn't feel that she was worthy of God's love. She was generous, hard working, sacrificing, sharing and concerned for all mankind. She loved music, beautiful art, her flowers, her cat and all of nature. Early on, she taught us the names of all of the birds in the area. She never took a job where she was not allowed to have time off to go to church on Sunday. She had jobs that were well beyond the strength of her tiny body. She worked in Mather Hospital, Republic Aircraft during WWII, Peerless Photo in Shoreham, and as a housekeeper for many different people. Before she was married, she worked as a bookkeeper and stenographer in Bayles Shipyard in Port Jefferson, which is where she met Daddy who also worked in the office there.

Daddy (John Thomas Martin Pettit) was a man of average build, a little paunchy, who was thirteen years my mother's senior. When he met Mom, he had been married before but, as far as I know, had no children. I say that because the name "Rose" appears written in on a list of heirs under his name in a Pettit family record. At any rate, he seemed to be the very type of person that Mom wanted to spend the rest of her life with. He was highly intelligent, quiet and gentle in nature – surprisingly so for a man who had left home at fourteen, traveled the country with a vaudeville group, played Shakespeare on many stages, lived in the developing west. Dad had married a woman named Marjorie. Mom knew about that and that she had died. But she didn't know about the drinking and wild side of his life until after she was married and Grandpa received a letter from one of Dad's family, telling Grandpa to "never let Ethel go away with John to live." How cruel. And she never did.

Dad's first lapse into drinking came when my mother was in Dr. King's hospital in Bay Shore giving birth to her first child, Muriel. He showed up quite drunk to welcome his new baby. Years went by and he didn't touch a drink until we were about eleven or twelve. He was working for Loper Brothers Co., managing their hardware and lumber store in Rocky Point when the drinking started again. During this time his father, Alexander Pettit of Brooklyn, died but Dad chose not to go to the funeral. I had never seen my Grandfather Pettit. Why? His brother Alfred, his sisters Edna and Edith kept in touch with us, but no one else in their family did. Dad would come home from work, go up into his room and stay there until everyone had finished dinner (usually about ten o'clock on Nana's schedule!), then Dad would come down to eat, alone, in the kitchen. He knew more about life than most and he was my mentor in learning about people – how to judge them by what they did and were, not by their color, religion (or lack of it), nationality or wealth.

Muriel was slight of build with light reddish brown hair and a lovely smile. She was not a healthy kid like Merle and I were. She stayed inside a great deal in those early days at Wildfields, reading constantly. She became an expert in history. She was quiet but stubborn, and her personality and Dad's often were in conflict. Her teachers loved her because she was such a good student and so well-behaved. She was closer to Mom than Merle or I ever became. We were more rugged and so we were together. Merle and I spent hours outside. We kicked a soccer ball around, climbed trees, raced through the fields, joked and laughed a lot. Muriel couldn't do many of the physical things that Merle and I were doing. Mom took her to St. Charles hospital in Port Jefferson for treatments as there was a problem with her spine. St. Charles dealt only with the problems of "crippled children" at that time and Dr. Childs saw Muriel for therapy.

I was outside watching all of nature's creatures performing their daily tasks, climbing into the forbidden hayloft of the old horse barn, or into the Wildfields attic to dream. I'd go through the huge homespun bags of old clothes and material, the boxes of dishes, Daddy's things from the West, and thought about the people who used or wore these things. I spent hours at the pond, hours with Dad on walks, playing with kittens, following Grandpa to the barns to watch him milk the cows, or just lying in the sun staring at the ever-changing heavens. At five, I wrote my first poem about black-eyed Susans. Mom always encouraged me to write and to draw and held little contests for the three of us.

Mom took care of Merle, but Uncle Nard (Louis Bernard Selleck) lived with us until he was remarried to Margaret V. Sorensen. They moved into the "Old House." Uncle Nard was a very outgoing man with definite opinions and a rather flamboyant nature, one of the "good old boys." He enjoyed life, especially his jazz band and loved playing in local taverns on Long Island for years. He and my Dad never got along for reasons unknown to me. Grandpa called his son "irresponsible" at times, but perhaps he was just overwhelmed with the loss of Ardell so early in their marriage. At any rate, he never stayed close to Merle – a fact that visibly upset her. Bernard was a good-looking man who liked the attention of the opposite sex. One time, one of his close friends shot at him through the bedroom window of the "Old House," thinking he was getting too friendly with his wife. Grandpa and Dad saw the man's car leave and knew who it was, but the matter was soon hushed as far as us kids were concerned.

Mom and Nana felt the pressure of Uncle Nard relinquishing his responsibility to his children, first of Merle and then of his two boys when Aunt Margaret became ill with tuberculosis. It was only natural that they would take in the children to care for them, but he did not offer to help. Mom would get angry but it made no difference. He slept late in the same room where two-year-old Burnell was crying in his crib, soaking wet. Sometimes I'd ask if I could go in and get him but was never allowed because Uncle Nard was asleep in there.

Years later, Merle felt that same anger when Grandpa asked her to pay back money that her father had borrowed and Grandpa needed. Merle refused. "That's his debt!" she told me.

But Bernard was a good musician and he probably would have rather been playing the piano than anything else in the world, anything.

So Merle came to Wildfields with her own built-in problems, and justifiably so. She had lost her mother. Her father had remarried and had not asked her to live with him. From being an only child, she had to enter a household where two other children were already established and then had to take direction from her aunt and her grandmother. Many were the times I heard Nana scolding her and Merle talking back. Within moments, Nana would go to her downstairs bedroom and out would come one of grandpa's belts. There would be a wild chase as Merle scurried up the stairs to her room. In retaliation, Merle needled and tormented Muriel and me, until one day I picked up a metal Victrola from my doll house and threw it at her from across my room. I missed her head by a hairs-breadth, and it hit the oak door before it falling to the floor. The mark must still be there and I remember it shamefacedly! As we grew older, we put aside our differences and lived in harmony, but the first years were rough. Mom dealt with Merle quite differently – as she did with all of us. She would talk with her quietly, reassuring her of her family status. Merle would lie on her bed for hours, reading, winding a handkerchief around her fingers and sucking her thumb. Once she had scarlet fever and Muriel and I would fill a basket (which Merle lowered from her bedroom window) with cookies, notes and trinkets. We were quarantined for weeks, a sign from the Health Department nailed to the front door. When Merle was well and the sign removed, all of her things and her room were fumigated. The secret of the goody basket was never revealed and we were all safe!

Down on the west slope of the hill beyond what was the "Carriage House" and is now the Nassakeag schoolyard, there was trailing pine. It is a plant that has round, flower-like greenery that grows vine-like close to the ground. Every year we decorated the mantle over the fireplace at Wildfields with greenery, a spray placed over the pendulum clock at the foot of the stairs, too. Now the play yard has taken away all such rare things – like the arbutus that grew in the nearby woods along the path where the school now stands.

Nana was never in any hurry to remove the pine from the mantle and there it stayed, dry and brittle, until early spring. One such spring day it caused quite a commotion. Aunt Margaret's brother, Russell, had come to visit her and he had made us three girls hoops out of a barrel. We were pushing these on Pond Path and having a wonderful time in front of the "Old House" and the corn crib to its south where Uncle Nard kept his car. Suddenly, my mother's voice pierced the air. She was leaning out of the upstairs sunporch window, shouting, "Get in the garage! Quick! Shut the doors! The bull is loose!" Terrified, we dropped our hoops in the road and did as we were told, our hearts pounding.

A quarter of a mile away, Thomas Hawkins kept a bull on his farm for breeding purposes. We had been told never to walk in his fields because this bull might charge after us. We had developed wild images of his "horrendous animal."

It seemed an eternity of waiting. We tried to peek out between the cracks of the old wooden doors, but could see nothing.

Finally, Russell appeared... laughing. Why did he think that such a frightening experience was funny? Well, it seems that Nana finally decided to undecorate the house. She had put all the greens in the fireplace and lit a fire. But she hadn't opened the flue. As smoke and flames shot out of the fireplace, she was desperately running back and forth from the kitchen with heavy pails of water to put out the fire. My mother, a nervous person at best, thought it was the pounding hooves of the bull that she heard. The scorched mantle and soaked rugs were reminders for some days to come of the *wild bull* charging through Wildfields.

The Christmas tree was another drawn-out project. For weeks during the fall, we girls combed the surrounding area for a suitably shaped cedar tree. It was always a cedar tree. There were no other evergreens growing here and no one ever bought a Christmas tree in all the years that I lived at Wildfields. How I envied the lovely spruce and fir in my friends' homes at Christmas! Once we three girls agreed on the tree for that year, we had to get Grandpa's consent to cut it down. Grandpa never refused us but we were never free of trepidation when we lined up before him to ask. He never took a physical part in the tree-trimming but sat quietly in his large chair, smoking his pipe, watching us with a smile pushing against the wrinkles of his face, happy to be a part of it. When we finally got the lights to work, there was a small grunt from the depths of his body somewhere, a "well done" grunt which we all understood. Ropes of tinsel bound the branches like scalloped ribbon. One by one the favorite ornaments were placed on the tree, followed by icicles. By now the excitement had no end. It was Christmas Eve and Mama always found the proper socks to hang on the fireplace. In the very bottoms of them, she placed a dime, an orange, a washcloth and a toothbrush. The rest was left up to the various "Santas" who contributed items collected throughout the year. We knew that at least one item would be something for our doll houses. One year "Santa" bought porcelain-faced dolls that fit into the furniture as families – all of this was left behind in Wildfields as we became adults and went off to college. Why did I come back to be so near to all these memories? Perhaps to realize that I had not – *never had* – a claim to any of it. Great Grandpa Ethelbert must have felt that others were living in *his* house. Only, it *was* his. None of Wildfields was ever really anything that belonged to us three girls. Grandpa, dear Grandpa, just let us all live there. I hope that Merle and Muriel finally figured that out also and put an end to the bitterness over possessions.

There was always a Christmas party at church. As children, we recited poems, sang carols. One year we did a short musical. I played the maid of the household and had a solo to sing. I recall how scared I was – up on the altar of the Setauket Presbyterian Church (est. 1660) – all alone. Mildred Ralph, the organist, played from the balcony from what seemed miles away. Following each program, the Strong family (of Strong's Neck) handed out oranges and a box of candy to each child from the Sunday school. Inside the box were hard candies and a few special chocolate creams. There was a large tree in the sanctuary, beautifully decorated, where we placed little red stockings filled with money for the poor.

Below the room where Daddy kept his things in the "Carriage House" was a small room next to where Grandpa kept his car. Uncle Nard had brought some of the old sections of the little post office where he had worked and had placed them there next to an old sleigh. There were several rows of mailboxes. Muriel and I loved to play in there, hiding little things in the boxes. One day we went there to play and pulled out a draw with a nest of tiny pink-bodied baby mice; I'd never seen such tiny animals. They looked like pink caterpillars. We carefully shut the drawer and sat quietly waiting to see the mother mouse. We waited and waited, shuffling our bodies on the seat of the sleigh. Finally, Muriel whispered, "Let's go," and we tip-toed out. We raced home to tell Mama and Nana what we had found and were sad when they told us that the mother mouse might not return since we had disturbed her nest. That night I prayed so hard that she would return to her babies. The next day we gulped down our breakfast and raced back to the "Carriage House." We did not touch the drawer, but we heard Mama Mouse scurrying about inside. It was an early lesson in the power of prayer.

Sometimes I lay on my stomach in the backyard near the milkhouse, fashioning tiny roads through and about the clumps of grass where a weed become a miniature tree. An ant would scurry along the path. Sometimes I took my porcelain doll-house dolls and made stick houses. Colored mints were bed pillows on mossy beds. Daddy bought us hammocks with metal stands. Merle and I turned the stands on their sides, pinned blankets to them and made them into tents. Inside we had dolls, cowboy outfits, guns, hats and apples – lots of apples to eat. One moment we were mothers; the next we were "riding the range." Rex, our collie, was always at our side. He died one spring after a pack of dogs attacked him in the woods beyond the pond. He often roamed with this pack, according to Uncle Nard, and probably was *dethroned* when he became too old. His wounds never healed and he had to be "put to sleep."

Uncle Nard loved animals and always had a dog or two at the "Old House." And there were always cats. The first that I remember was Tommy, a sleek tiger-striped tabby that Dad found abandoned when he was the manager of Loper Bros. Hardware Store and lumberyard. Loper's owned several cottages in that area which were summer rentals. It was one of Dad's responsibilities at summer's end to inspect each one for needed repairs and to turn the water and electricity off. In one cottage, he found Tommy, left behind, hungry and fearful. Tommy stayed at the store with Dad until we begged to bring him home. He had an extra toe on each front foot and could hold a pencil. Tommy was about nineteen years old when Mom had to put him to sleep. She bought him cans of mackerel and mixed it with bread; she drove to Aunt Aurelia's old home where Kapps now lived and bought some of the horsemeat they sold. Cat food in cans was available then. Dad bought him cans of sardines. He was a beautiful cat that gave Mom comfort long after we had all gone away to college and Dad had died.

I had a Maltese cat named Midge who had her kittens in my bed, my first experience with a "mother's role" in bringing life into this world. I watched her pull the sacks off the newborn kittens and then wash them tenderly as each appeared from her body.

When I returned to Wildfields in 1967, and built my home there beyond the clothesline and the hedges, we had Moe with us. He had a steel pin in his leg from an encounter with a car in Middletown, N.Y. but was still chasing his tail and climbing trees at seventeen. Since then we've had many cats.

One of our cats, Lucius, sat on the counter watching Leonard (my son) make a tuna sandwich, but never intruding. One May evening he was hit by a car and died. A few months later, Sam joined us – probably Leonard's favorite. We kept him inside and he was Leonard's constant buddy, sleeping on the couch or nearby when Len couldn't sleep. He was the biggest cat I've ever seen. He was soft and gray with a white bib and white front paws. Soon after, we got another of Carol's cats (Lucius was also one) a sable Burmese named Elizabeth. I really didn't want an exotic, noisy cat, but she wasn't able to mix well with Carol's many animals, so I took her. She grew to be the dearest pet I've ever had. At fifteen years, she developed a brain tumor and I lost her just a few days before my last major surgery. The night before I took her to the vet to be put down, she lay against my cheek, licking away my tears.

Now we have Stripuss and Gracie – two tabbies who were strays and are indoor/outdoor cats. Between Sam's lifetime and now, we gave away Lionel (renamed John Wesley by his new owner, Elsie Kolff, because I gave him to her at church) and Alexandria, who died of seizures.

Pets were always a big part of our lives because we seldom strayed far from Wildfields, although when we were little kids there was an annual summer excursion to Montauk Point. It was at least a two-car event. Grandpa, Nana, Mama, Merle, Muriel and I were in one; Aunt Aurelia, Auntie Squires, Cousin Charles and Cousin Edith were in the other. It was a long, long drive, broken by our expectation of seeing Long Island's Big Duck, which was then just east of Riverhead. It was a landmark, a beacon, a "thank God, we're halfway there" or a "halfway home" marker. In the early morning we helped pack the picnic lunch and put in cups and napkins and silverware. We took gallon jugs of homemade lemonade, hard-boiled eggs, tuna sandwiches and cookies. Grandpa always found the same big rock before we got to the end of the Island (there were no houses for miles) and he pulled off the road into the sand. We spread blankets for the picnic and were finally allowed to walk down a poison ivy-lined path to the Atlantic Ocean, but were told not to go in – it was *too dangerous.*

Once or twice a year we were taken into New York City on a shopping spree to the big department stores. Grandpa went with Mom and us so that he could order his high-buttoned shoes someplace downtown. We three girls were with Mom for what seemed like hours of "don'ts" from my anxious, worried mother. Before we even left home, it began. New York City was to her a den of "white slavery, thieves, racing automobiles, vile drunken men and painted women."

We would leave from Stony Brook Railroad Station after buying tickets, listening to the clicking telegraph machine and waiting with excitement for the huffing, coal-burning train to come around the bend from Setauket. The train would start with a jerk, smoke billowing past the window, whistle wailing.

Sometimes our journey was to Rutherford, New Jersey, where we stayed with Uncle Ray and Aunt Una. Usually that was when Merle went to her Aunt Leslie's. Grandpa would drive her to Plainview while we took the train to Rutherford. Aunt Una Norris was Nana's youngest sister. More frequently, we went to Manorville which was closer than the Jersey relatives. Here is where the Burghardt part of the family comes in.

A few years ago, Cousin Eva and Herbert Carter's daughter, Dencie, phoned me from her home in Bellport. I hadn't seen or talked to her since I was a young adult, probably when I was in my twenties. I took down the information about directions to her home on North Paquatuck Avenue; Dave Selleck and I discussed going there. I have such pleasant memories of Dencie at Cousin Eva's in Center Moriches.

Two days ago, the paper with the information scrawled on it fell from my address book, landing on the kitchen floor. I put it up on the refrigerator. When Dave returned from a trip to Michigan to be with his mother and Burnell, I'd ask him if he'd still like to go there to visit Dencie if she was still here and able to have company.

A few minutes later the phone rang. It was Dencie! *Who can explain such happenings?*

"It was meant to be," said Dencie, who at eighty-four, lives in a small home with a cerebral palsied man to help with lawn work and snow shoveling. Friends get groceries because her eyesight keeps her from driving. Dencie's great-grandmother (and my great-great grandmother) was Eliza Burghardt, whose maiden name was Troll or Troal; records vary. She was born in London, England, on June 14, 1819, died at age forty-seven on July 18, 1866, and was buried in Patchogue, Long Island. Eliza married George Burghardt who was a fur trader who settled here. He returned to England on business after his marriage, taking Eliza with him. It was while they were in London that my great-grandmother, Ruth Susanna, was born. When she was six weeks old, they returned to America. Ruth Susanna had an older sister named Adelaide Eva Drew who was Dencie's grandmother. Her sisters, Maria and Laura, and her brother, Charles, will be mentioned elsewhere. There was also a sister Eliza (Aunt Liza) who married a Steven Allen; and a brother John, who lived in Brooklyn and owned a large moving business on Furman Ave. before he moved to Sayville. His daughter Julia married William Weeks of Patchogue. Julia only lived to be thirty-six years of age. One of her children, Edna, became a nurse at Belleview Hospital in Manhattan. Her first husband died in the flu epidemic of 1918, and her second husband was a Dr. Henry Weston.

Adelaide Eva Drew was the dear old lady who lived in Manorville and whom we often visited. Aunt Eva, as we all called her, married Andrew Davis, a streetcar conductor. Their son Charles lived in Floral Park with his wife Mae. They had one child, also named Eva Drew. Aunt Eva and Uncle Andrew had already named their only daughter Eva Drew, born 1880. She married Herbert Carter and lived in Center Moriches. They had three daughters: Viola who married Charles Smith and they lived in Calverton as farmers; Marie who married Howard Johnson (who did not own the restaurants, but worked in a bank in Center Moriches where Cousin Herbert had worked); and a third daughter who was Dencie, who married Edward Rogers. Their first son died in infancy. Their second son, David, is a teacher in Center Moriches High School. Their third child was a girl, Colleen, whose first husband died and whose second is John Gilmartin.

I would not have had the Burghardt information if it were not for Aunt Margaret Selleck. I didn't realize that she was compiling it until one day she asked my help with it.

Eliza Troll Burghardt was great-great grandmother to David, Burnell, Merle, Muriel and me. So, all of you descendants, please take it from here. If you want a copy of what we compiled with regard to the Burghardts, just ask. It includes all the Burnells, through her daughter Ruth Susanna.

Grandpa, Nana, Mom, Merle, Muriel and I would visit Cousins Eva and Herbert. Their home bordered one of the canals, and of course we kids were saturated with admonishments from Mom not to go near the water. Cousin Herbert kept a boat at his backyard dock on the canal beyond his barn/garage. It was the beautiful home that I remember best. Usually Viola's daughter, Doris, was at her grandmother's if she knew we were coming. The back staircase was my greatest fascination – like a secret passage to our bedroom above if we stayed overnight, which we girls did sometimes.

Once there was a block party that we all went to and we stayed out later than I ever had before. I suddenly became nauseous with the summer's heat, the excitement, the swirling dances, the food. I left my mark in the grass at the roadside before they took me home, where I went to bed, shivering and wishing Mom had stayed. The quiet and solitude of Wildfields were welcome the next day. Everyone at Cousin Eva's was good to me, but home is home.

There was always music at Wildfields. No matter what sorrow or worry was taking place, there was music. Nana listened to Milton Cross announce the opera and classical music on the radio. On Sundays we heard the Mormon Tabernacle Choir. Dad sang his vaudeville songs, Mom sang her hymns and lilting songs of the day. Uncle Nard played piano, all the popular music of the day. Merle became an accomplished pianist and added Mozart, Chopin, Beethoven, Bach and others to her repertoire. Grandpa played the mandolin, Muriel the guitar, and I the piano, playing by ear as Uncle Nard had taught me. We were surrounded by art and music and good books. When I was five I began writing poetry and from then on, Mom sent my poetry to children's magazines.

Sometimes my writing was published in "Children's Digest" and "St. Nicholas Magazine" (1873-1941). In high school we all worked on the school paper. Muriel wrote funny articles, turning her initials M.E.S into her pen name, Emmy Ess. In college I was elected to Alpha Sigma Omicron, the honorary literary society, and in my senior year edited the literary magazine. When I was in eighth grade my teacher, Mrs. Hendrickson, asked us to do a project on what we wanted to do when we grew up. Without hesitation, I said I wanted to be a writer. I still do!

As we grew older, we realized how much more we had than so many others. There were many, in fact most, families living in poverty on Chicken Hill. That section of Setauket lay on the top of the hill behind the Methodist Church and on the corner of Old Town Road west. Many Polish families lived there. and blacks mingled with whites. All of the children came to school with us, of course, and for some it was the start of bigotry, for others the introduction to liberalism.

When the Great Depression hit, things grew really tough, especially for these families. We all shared our clothes with less fortunate families and our recycled garments often appeared on a friend who hadn't grown as fast as one of us. Children came to school without coats in the winter, with shoes whose soles were tied on with string, with ragged, torn clothing impossible to mend. Most of the Polish families were Catholic and had large families. The large black families were there also. By the time I was in high school, my own family was hard pressed for money. Dad was ill, Mom went to work in private homes. When I was fifteen I worked all summer at the Stony Brook School and later at Gregson's Lodge on weekends until 2 a.m.

Left on my own, I arose just in time to slap jam on two slices of bread and wrap it in waxed paper, dress, grab my books, and run for the bus to take me to school. Without any breakfast, I was starving long before noon and kept pulling off bites of bread and sneaking them from my desk to eat. By lunchtime, there was no lunch left. After this went on for weeks – or months – my best friend, Marjorie Heinz, began bringing an extra sandwich which she was "just too full to eat." Made on her mom's, Millie Heinz's, homemade bread, it was manna from Heaven.

God bless Millie and Marge for all the meals and kindness that they nourished me with. Their home on Bayview Avenue, Setauket was as familiar as Wildfields.

Nana was like that, too. When she was alive she gave us so much more than just a home. She rarely felt well, but never seemed to complain.

When Grandpa brought the milk pails in from the barn, Nana strained the milk through a cloth into large pans which were then covered and placed in the ice box in the milk house. When she was ready, I helped her skim the rich cream from the top of the pans and then helped make pot cheese or butter. I didn't like the smell of the warm milk, and to this day I am repulsed by melting butter. The pot cheese was rolled into large grapefruit-sized balls, wrapped in waxed paper, and taken out to the ice box. Before Grandpa bought the electric refrigerator, the ice truck would come and the iceman would cut off huge blocks of ice which he weighed and then, using tongs, took to the ice box. In fact, this went on long after the Frigidaire arrived, for the milk pans were too cumbersome for the indoor refrigerator.

In the summer, Nana made gallons of root beer which sat on a shelf in the Wildfields pantry. Some kind of root went into the bottling of each jug and yeast was added to the water. It took several days before it was ready.

Mom and Nana made apple jelly in the fall. Apples were peeled and cut for applesauce (which was canned and stored in the cellars) and for pies. The peelings were cooked and hung in a cloth bag from the towel rack next to the store. The juice dropped through the cloth very slowly into a pan below and then was cooked with pectin and sugar into clear, amber jelly.

Nana made the decisions as to what was to be done in the household – and when. "What do *you* think, Mama?" I'd hear my mother say. In spite of the never-ending picking, preparing, cooking and canning of food, we all had fun. In fact, it was fun doing it.

We played Parcheesi, Old Maid, checkers, tiddlywinks, jacks, croquet and jump rope. Nana, with her sisters Aunt Una and Aunt Aurelia, all believed in the powers of the Ouija board and as we three girls grew older, we spent hours fooling with it, but never believed in it. Aunt Una was visiting one time when the women brought out the Ouija board which spelled out "Una has trouble at home."

When she returned home to Rutherford, New Jersey, Una found that her house had been burglarized. Imagine how that fueled their belief! Miss Medd, one of our social studies teachers, told us that the Ouija board was the work of the devil. Personally, we all thought it stupid.

I just drove back to Storybook Lane down Pond Path from Route 347 (Nesconset Highway). When we first moved back to Setauket in 1967, the Long Island Expressway only went as far as Smithtown and we always got off there and came down the bypass (Route 347) to Pond Path. Now the Long Island Expressway goes as far as Riverhead.

We never called Pond Path by that name when we grew up here. It was just the road to Nassakeag or "the Setauket road."

Today. it seems as though, overnight, the dull late-summer foliage has taken on its last "hurrah," a renewal before the reality of winter sets in. The bright red of maple contrasts with the rusty oak and yellow goldenrod. The most beautiful of seasons taunts us to watch before the skeletons appear.

Along the patch of road on the west side of Pond Path between Campus Drive and Cornwallis Street are many memories. I can feel Dad's presence. It was my favorite of all favorite spots on our land. Dad would take me by the hand and walk me down Pond Path from Wildfields to the old Woodlot Road – a narrow dirt passageway which wound into the summer woods and from which Grandpa had his firewood cut. There was always the sweet smell of summer greenery and damp moss. The trees towered far above me and I was soon lost to all bearings, all turns, all space. Dad would hum and sing old show tunes from his days in vaudeville, "Daisy, Daisy, On a Bicycle Built For Two," "The Sidewalks of New York," "Sweet Rosie O'Grady," or as quickly, change and quote parts of Shakespeare from his acting days. I loved him so much and I knew we'd soon come to my spot. There it would be – like a palace door opening into the throne room – a beautiful, sunny glen in the middle of the forest. Sunlight streamed down between the trees onto the soft green grass and patches of pure white sand. Asters bloomed and small white birches edged the glen like children waiting to play. My heart carries the peace of this place to this day. I've done an oil painting of it – as much as memory serves me. Houses now nestle against the ridge beyond it, and even where the glen lay. The development is a torment.

Dad and I did many things together. No one else in the family seemed to be able to have a decent relationship with him. He was so bright and knowledgeable and so full of interesting stories of his life before Setauket. But here was a hidden side which came to me years after his death.

I knew that Dad had been married before to a Marjorie. She died, I believe, on the West Coast somewhere. Dad had traveled with a vaudeville acting company where he actually worked with George M. Cohan at one time. He often sang to me and he once told me that his throat was damaged in a scene from King Lear when he played a slave or soldier (I've forgotten which) and was dragged by a body harness off the stage. The harness slipped and choked him and his voice projection was never the same again, he told me. Anyhow, that's where Marjorie entered his life. But then there was Rosa, an opera singer whom he never mentioned but whose personal belongings, like her autograph book and clippings, he carried with him to Wildfields. The name Rose appeared handwritten on the list of heirs as I've mentioned – above all other names. I wrote to every county clerk whose town appeared in the album or was listed in her clippings or her travels, but never made a connection. Were they ever married? Was Rose her child? No one in the family would tell Muriel or me. Dad's sister Edith told us to "leave your memories as they are." Aunt Lillian, another sister, whom we finally met at age ninety-two, would not even discuss Dad in any way. We drove her past his Setauket burial site in the Presbyterian churchyard and she just turned her head away. Such pain. What did he do to them all? Grandpa had received that letter. We probably will never know. Perhaps it's just as well.

Aunt Lillian lived in Calverton, Long Island, and we *discovered* her when Aunt Edna died and Lillian's son, a lawyer from Bar Harbor, Maine, contacted Muriel and me. I had never met him before he arrived in his Mercedes to go over Dad's sister Edna's will. He was not the executor, just an advisor. Dad's brother Alex had lived in Northport, Long Island, and we didn't know him, either. His grandson Robert Harned was the executor.

Clifford showed me the list of heirs. Someone else was there to notarize the papers and so I felt it better not to ask about Rose or Rosa. I'd find out another time, I believed. It was then that I learned that Aunt Lillian lived – and had for years – just a few towns away in Calverton. Her daughter, my first cousin, lived in Setauket until her death. I had never seen her!

When Muriel and I learned of Aunt Lillian's address, we set out to find her. With Muriel's daughter, Margaret, and my son Leonard, we traveled to Calverton and found her home on River Road, high up on a hillside covered with azaleas (which she had planted and transplanted at age ninety!). She came to the door and wasn't going to let us in, believing we were Jehovah's Witnesses, but when we said we were her brother John's daughters, she took us in with open arms – even fed us lunch. We brought her back to my home in Setauket for dinner but Dad was no longer a part of *her* family.

Almost two years later, Aunt Lillian died.

Muriel then wrote Aunt Edith and we were to visit her in Syracuse, New York, but Muriel's battle with cancer intervened and we never did go. She also died a few years later. I kept in touch with Roberta (granddaughter of my father's brother, Alexander) and still do – but no one has ever offered any explanation of the family's problem with Dad. Roberta's father died when she was very young; her brother was killed in an auto accident; her mother Edna Pettit has died; Muriel is gone. Roberta and I remain of all of the known living relatives of John Thomas Martin Pettit.

Dad and his six brothers and sisters grew up in Brooklyn, New York, where his father, Alexander Pettit, owned a brickyard. After he left home at fourteen he spent much time in California and Nevada. When he came back east, he worked in an auto plant in Newburgh doing bookkeeping and then gravitated to Long Island where he was employed in the office of Bayles Shipyard. During his youth, he apparently had serious drinking problems, but they had been controlled for years and Mom had no idea that they existed. When we lived in the "Old House" the days of wooden ships ended and Bayles Shipyard in Port Jefferson eventually closed. Dad took an office job in Brooklyn at Gaseau-Tompkins. Mom would weave scraps of mattress cretonnes into rugs. Dad and Grandpa traveled the Long Island Rail Road and walked through the woods to the Stony Brook station. Dad returned for weekends only. By the time Grandpa had returned and built Wildfields, Dad was again working nearby. Grandpa got him a job with his old friend Arthur Lopes in their Port Jefferson lumber yard. When they opened a branch hardware store and lumberyard in Rocky Point, Dad was made manager. At first, Grandpa drove Dad to and from work at Rocky Point – twelve miles each way, as Dad didn't drive. What a Saint Grandpa was!

Dad was at *least* fifty-five years of age before he finally got his license, and he was always a terrible driver. His first car was a small Studebaker with only one seat (the driver's, of course) in front and a small, crowded back seat. Dad put a wooden box on the floor next to him so we could ride with him.

Every weekend until I was out of school, I spent some time with Dad – I knew things were not right; his attitude toward the family was wrong. He was drinking and was often brought home from work by his helper, Godfrey Petersen, too drunk to even climb the stairs alone. Without a license, he would ask me to drive him to local bars. I'd sit and wait for him in the car. Sometimes he visited a black woman on Chicken Hill. I wonder now why no one cared about this, but Mom was away from home working as maid or cook, or both, and Grandpa did not interfere.

Finally Dad got too ill to work. Muriel stayed home the year after she graduated from high school and kept the house. She got her license and drove to school daily for a postgraduate course in typing. We ate every casserole known to man. Bacon was the only meat. Grandpa wished for more, but it was the best we could do. In the summers we worked at the Stony Brook Boys School. Dad grew weaker and weaker. He had never mixed with the family or our friends. He went nowhere with us as a family – not even to see us graduate. I was eighth-grade and high school valedictorian, but he wasn't there to hear my boring speeches, the first on the whaling industry on Long Island and the second the usual "We go forward, blah-blah-blah..." We were in plays, shows, concerts, club events and more. He never came to see us. Merle had solo parts more than once. Mom and Grandpa were there ...*never* Dad.

After I graduated from high school, both Muriel and I entered the State Teachers College at New Paltz, where we worked in separate homes for our room and board. Mom was still working away from home. Dad and Grandpa (an unlikely alliance) were at home. Years before (1928) Grandpa put in an electric refrigerator and with it came a set of Depression ware and a set of small 5" x 7" encyclopedias. Nana gave the encyclopedias to Dad and he read and reread them. Thanks to Dave Selleck, they are now in my home, as is Brownie, the stuffed dog that Grandpa won for us.

Dad's last year of life was a sad one. He was lonely and sick. That early summer, Dr. Squires told us that he only had a few months to live. Muriel was working in New York City or upstate – I can't recall which – as a dietitian. Merle was in Brooklyn at St. John's Hospital. I worked days at Stony Brook School as a waitress and a barmaid at Gregson's in Stony Brook weekend nights. I came home to help Dad eat and get through another night. He taught me to make lentil soup which sustained him. His breathing became worse; his legs and body began to fill with fluid. In mid-August Merle came for a week's vacation and gave him shots of morphine. Before she returned to Brooklyn, she taught me how to give them. His legs were twice their size, but his arms were just hanging flesh. I had a terrible time getting the needles in. For days after his death, his arms and legs floated by me in dreams. He would call me to sit in front of him and read the 23rd Psalm and he'd watch my breathing and try to breathe when I did. "Yea, though I walk through the valley of the shadow of death, I will fear no evil: for thou [art] with me; thy rod and thy staff they comfort me." Finally he lapsed into a coma. I sat on the bed, exhausted. He was propped up in the Morris chair. When his labored breathing ceased, I fell asleep. This song had ended on August 27, 1942.

All of Dad's mysteries, his secrets, his addictions and his dreams were not important anymore. His brilliant mind was at rest and now he's with Mom and Marjorie (and maybe, Rosa).

I still miss him.

As children, we were all an integral part of the Setauket Presbyterian Church. We faithfully attended Sunday School (earned our pins each year), church, Bible School and all sang in the choir led by Mildred Ralph, the organist.

We sat on Mama and Daddy's bed every Saturday evening learning and reciting our Bible verses for the next day. One Children's Day, we sang as a trio, "Just a little pansy." Mom coached us and watched with pride as we stood before the congregation, a bouquet of pansies in our hands, bright against our pure white dresses trimmed with white satin ribbons. The tune is still clear in my head, but not the words.

When Mom came to live with Vic and me in Florida, we bought pansies for her every Mother's Day. This was true wherever we lived.

On Saturday nights we helped Daddy shine our patent leather shoes for Sunday School the next day. All but Daddy and Nana attended church where Grandpa was a elder. The Strong family from Strong's Neck was the backbone of the church, financially and otherwise. They influenced us in every phase of our growing up. Miss Bessie (Elizabeth D. Strong) taught the primary group. We were barely able to climb the steep stairs; our class was held in the balcony. It seems ludicrous now, but in those days, four- and five-year-olds sat still on the wooden benches while Miss Bessie went over the lesson, taught us to pray, and in her frail, wispy, off-key voice, taught us children's songs about Jesus. Miss Bessie was a thin-faced women who wore high-buttoned black shoes, black cotton stockings, a long dark shirt, and long-sleeved blouses with a high neck and a tiny straw hat rimmed with flowers perched on top of her head above the bun which wound her long hair in the back.

We looked down upon the altar and empty pews waiting for the adults to come to church. The organ was left of us as we faced the open sanctuary.

Miss Bessie wrote poetry, most of which had religious themes and, when wintering in Florida, would send Mom copies of her little poetry booklets which she had published. One read:

> "Lord Jesus take these messages
> Given to this heart of mine
> Often through study of thy word.
> Bless all that is wholly thine.
> These glimpses are of eighty years.
> There bits from my life's story;
> Forgive, dear lord, what is amiss.
> To Thee be all the glory."

In December 1958 shoe wrote Mom from Bradenton, Florida. "February 26th I celebrated my 84th birthday. My brother and his wife came to be here for a week helping to make the day happier.

"Sister Kate's eyes are no better, but she keeps cheerful and finds comfort in radio and taking books and several cages of tropical birds as pets, teaches her Social Studies class of boys and goes to church on good Sundays."

When in the Setauket church somewhere, we could hear the noisy boys in Miss Kate's class. She always taught the boys and was herself the *tomboy* of the three sisters. When all the other parishioners arrived in cars, Kate rode to church from Strong's Neck in her horse-drawn buggy which she pulled into the shed on the west side of the church driveway. She wore long shirts of coarse cotton, sometimes held together with a horse blanket pin (much to our amusement, of course!). Miss Kate was the greatest storyteller I've ever known. In the summer when we were at Bible school, she gathered us all at her feet as she sat outside on the front steps and told Bible stories. She made it all seem so simple and good and so rewarding. "Jesus," she told us, "gave us the where-with-all to have a *world* that was *wonderful*, because He loved us."

We had no idea then how hard it would be to make a truly *wonderful world*.

As we grew older, we moved up to Miss Carolyn Strong's class. She was the daughter of Mr. and Mrs. John Strong. Her mellow voice and easy laughter made us all want to be good. We had picnics at the Strong Mansion on Strong's Neck – the waters of Setauket Bay lay at the foot of the yard. Caroline's mother taught the adult Bible class. She had a sister Helen Ridgeway, who lived there also. I always wondered why Mrs. John Strong looked so sad. Miss Helen was more outgoing. She also wore the high-buttoned shoes, long skirts, blouses with high necks and beautiful cameos at her throat. They all wore their hair pulled back in a bun and dressed in an era long gone by, still proudly holding on to the prestige that had been theirs for generations.

Miss Cornelia taught us as teenagers. She lived with Kate and Bessie in their father's home. Selah and John are just vague images to me. When Bessie left for Bradenton each winter in her later years, Cornelia went to Pasadena, particularly to be there for the Tournament of Roses. Kate more often stayed at home.

You certainly could say (pun intended) that they had a Strong religious influence on our lives. As pre-teenagers, we still attended Bible school every summer. Mom was going to be sure that we were, and would remain, good Christians. We had no objections; we even walked all the way to the church and back at times. We enjoyed it.

Dr. Gaebelein was the Head Master at what was then the Stony Brook Prep School for Boys. His unmarried sister-in-law was Miriam Medd who lived in the family home in Old Field and kept in close touch with her sister, Dorothy Gaebelein and her family. Miss Medd had an infectious, positive quality about her. She had us trembling youngsters get up and witness on the altar one Sunday morning. Never was the power of the Holy Spirit more moving in our lives. She took us from childhood beliefs to the reality of applying them in our daily lives. She gave me my first Concordance after learning all the books of the Bible in their order. She added to the fact that we had parents and grandparents who loved us and gave us a healthy start on our journey toward heaven. And she made us understand that it wouldn't be easy.

When we were teenagers we all sang in the church choir. It also gave us another dimension to our social life. The choir was led by Mildred Ralph and was made up of all teenagers except for one adult, Florence Baldwin – who was our school secretary. It didn't take us long to figure out that Florence was also enriching her social life by going to choir rehearsal and was meeting a local, very good-looking married man there. After rehearsal they would get in Florence's car and drive off toward Strong's Neck. One evening, our usually fertile minds up-to-no-good decided we should plant a bra on the back seat of the "gentleman's" car. Off came my raggedy bra amidst the usual gales of laughter and into his car it went.

At the next week's rehearsal, he lined us all up outside, looked us over carefully, and handed me back my bra. Even then, my big boobs got me into trouble.

This gentleman had a young son who grew up to be President Nixon's speech writer.

Due to Dad's illness, Mom had gone to work in private homes at Camp Upton, Mather Hospital, Peerless Photo. Muriel filled in at Wildfields as manager and housekeeper for Grandpa, Dad and me.

After I graduated from high school, Muriel and I both went to New Paltz to college to train to be teachers. Muriel stayed for the first semester, working in a private home taking care of a physician's two children. She decided teaching was not for her and returned to Wildfields and later attended dietetic school in New York City. I remained at New Paltz (then a state teacher's college) to work in a professor's home, doing all of the household chores except cooking. I gave up every free period to do this for my room and board. It was 1940-1944 and we would soon be facing the horrors of friends shot down at sea or killed in action on the ground. There were boys we had dated, danced with, laughed with: Orlando (Buddy) Lyons, Jack Gillard, Billy Weston, Anthony Matusky, Jim Pfeiffer. The knowledge of death is like taking a bullet to your heart, and this happened over and over. How do young people survive this? Do they? We had to try very hard, and sometimes we made a mess of it.

The closest friends that I made at New Paltz have been my friends for life. In my sophomore year I moved out of the private home and into Coutant House where my old friend from Setauket, Marge Heinz, joined me as my roommate. Ten of us lived in that house converted into a dorm, with elderly Maggie Newton as our house mother. Sometimes we all cooked together. Sometimes we ate in two or threes, or alone. None of us had enough money to provide decent meals. We had one coffeepot – an eight cup Drip-o-Later. The first morning cup was fine, but from then until evening we just ran hot water through the same dregs. We washed all of our clothes and bed linens by hand; cleaned our rooms which consisted of two single beds, two desks, two chairs, a sink and two closets. We used orange crates for extra storage, sometimes covered with flowered cloth. We all went by our last names: Cuddy, Lynch, Sally (for Salvador), Beggie (for Bigos), Pet (for Pettit), Heinz, etc. I still find it difficult to call them by their first names.

It was the era of the Big Bands and we danced at the corner store, or in the gym, or at some bar out on the highways. We jitter-bugged to the juke box – girls with girls when our men all went to war. We played bridge and drank bumpers of beer and smoked cigarettes at ten cents a pack. We shared the fear and loneliness that the war brought to us. We all married almost as soon as we graduated from college and sent our husbands off to lands we had never known. When, or if, they returned, many marriages failed simply because they shouldn't have been in the first place.

When I was a junior in college, Dad died. I was nineteen. He wouldn't be coming to my college graduation, either.

The war was hard on everyone. We probably suffered less than many, having no men in the family young enough to go to war or old enough. No one in our immediate or extended families died in World War II. But our friends did.

The first came before the draft had called any of them. Muriel's high school class graduated in 1939 and chose as their class motto, "Live today as though you were to die tomorrow." Their interpretation was not as intended. They chose it because of the war and the possibility of early death. So, live it up!

One night, Bob Darling, Jack Gillard, and Bill Weston were driving along the Long Island south shore at a rate too fast for logic. A collision occurred. Bob flew through the windshield, severing his carotid artery. He died that night. Bill was driving and as long as he lived (which wasn't much longer, thanks to the war in Europe) he could not erase the memory of that night. Both Jack and his cousin Bill were killed in the war a few years later. Bill's mom had been an opera singer and he lived with her on Hawkins Avenue while his dad stayed at the fire house as a dispatcher. Millie Heinz told me how she heard the screams when Poppy Weston learned of her son's death. And then silence for days. Millie took soup and other food to her, but she would not talk to anyone and, as far as I know, Poppy Weston never sang again.

I had dated Billy many times, often double-dating with Walter Eichacker who later became a local doctor. But Bill's true love was always Merle's friend, Leila.

The nearest house to Wildfields and the homestead was at least a quarter of a mile away. At the foot of the hill on Pond Path was the Matusky farm. It faced the entrance to St. George's Golf and Country Club, which is still there. Unfortunately, the Matusky's home is gone. In 1993 Mary Matusky (now Mary Mattwell, having had the family change its name) sold the last parcel of the farm to the developers who had already built several homes surrounding the old farmhouse. The house itself was built – or put together from other small homes, by Samuel Hawkins who was our (Merle, Muriel, David, Burnell and me) great-great-great-great-great grandfather.

Keep in mind what I've told you about the weirdness in our family! Here it goes again.

Robert and Mary; son Zachariah; son Eleazer; son Alexander – that line I've traced for you to the "Old House.." Eleazer had another son named Samuel who married a Mary Green and farmed at Nassakeag. They are also buried in the Hawkins cemetery on Pond Path. Samuel and Alexander were in the fourth generation of Hawkins in America. Samuel and Mary had seven children, one of which was Zopher. Kate Strong told a story about Zopher that is fascinating.

Zopher lived in the Hawkins house across from the now St. George's golf course. Many friendly Setauket Indians lived in the area and Zopher had many friends among them. But one day, hostile Indians captured Zopher and he lived with them for three years, married an Indian, but eventually escaped by using the skills of following stars that his friendly Indian friends taught him. He hid in a hollow log until the Indians stopped searching for him and found his way home. Later, he became involved in a battle near the Setauket Mill Pond with the British. His friend, Arthur Smith, dropped from a bullet and lay at his side, but Zopher fooled the British with an old Indian trick of lying face down to feign death. He later married and had six children. He and his wife are buried on Pond Path in the Hawkins cemetery.

Samuel and Mary also had a son, John – who married Mary (Newton) Hawkins. They had a son also named Zopher. John's wife Mary was the daughter of Simeon and Elizabeth ("Carriage House" was their home). Mary was Merritt's sister. Zopher's second wife bore him eight children, one of whom was Ebenezer, our great-great grandfather, and who married Sarah Ann.

So... going back in time:

Grandpa Ethelbert m. Elsie Burnell his mom, Hester Anna m. Ethelbert Selleck, her mom Sarah Ann m. Ebenezer Hawkins, her father Merritt Hawkins m. Anna Hawkins, his father Simeon Hawkins ("Old House") m. Elizabeth Hawkins.

Ebenezer Hawkins m. Sarah Ann Hawkins, his father Zopher m. Mary (daughter of Simeon), his father John m. Mary Newton, his father Samuel m. Mary Green. And it was Samuel who built the house at the joining of Pond Path and Lower Sheep Pasture Road across from the golf course.

"Oh what a tangled web..."

When my cousin David Selleck learned that this house was to be demolished, he contacted Beverly Tyler of the Three Village Historical Society, and proceedings were started immediately to try and save the house. The builder cooperated and extended the time before he would build there as long as it was before the first frost. It was too costly to move the house, so Beverly, David and other interested parties took it apart piece by piece, saving the old solid beams to rebuild it somewhere else. Dave came out to Wildfields on Saturday to help. Some worked daily.

The old Samuel Hawkins house is gone and a new two-story Victorian style home is in its place. Mary (Matusky) Mattwell lives behind it in her newer home. Her ten brothers and sisters are scattered about. Anthony died a World War II hero – Mary put several of the siblings through college and had them change their names to Mattwell. She herself taught school in Nassau or Queens for many years. I still remember going with Grandpa up the long lane to that farmhouse to buy bushels of lima beans to can. Mrs. Matusky, a poor hard-working Polish immigrant would come out of the well-worn door, her head in a bandana, an apron tied about her waist. She kept her children neatly dressed. After her husband died her son, Joe, quit school to help work the farm. Recently his daughter, Lorraine, told me that her father spent a year living in the old schoolhouse once located at the end of their driveway. He couldn't get along with his father whom he labeled cold and severe. Farm grains, products, and tools were often stored in the old schoolhouse when the Matusky's lived there. The building has since been moved and is a part of the Museums at Stony Brook.

Lorraine Mattwell passed away in the winter of 1997.

It is six in the morning. Bright streaks of sunshine are painted across the yard. As the earth falls into summer green, strewing its blossoms everywhere, I think of Mama and her gardens filled with flowers. My granddaughters, Lisa and Michele, came from Albany and planted foxglove, snapdragons, snowdrops, marigolds, petunias and impatiens. The perennial gaillardias are hiding the johnny-pump-ups in their rush to show off and take over the garden by the front door patio. Mama taught us to identify these flowers and so many more: larkspur, phlox, cosmos, carnations, zinnias – the list goes on! It was a very English garden that she grew and she taught us to weed and cultivate the rows and then to pick them and arrange the flowers into beautiful bouquets. These were often taken to friends and shut-ins. Grandpa grew the dahlias. Their rich, beautiful colors were like velvet gowns. Each fall I helped him dig up the tubers and bring baskets full to the cellar storage room next to the crookneck squash. That was a sad time for me, when leaves had fallen and left trees bare and the flowers were all but gone. It seemed an endless wait for spring to bring back the long rows of jonquils and the blooms on the lilacs and syringa bushes.

On Main Street in Setauket there is a huge rock. Going north toward the ponds it is on the left side of the road. Thank God "progress" hasn't bull dozed it away. Right next to this road, Mr. Wallace had his little store. Mama or Grandpa and we girls would go into his store to buy butter or cheese which we cut from big wheels and then weighed on his counter scales. Then he wrapped it in oiled paper and tied it with a string, which hung down over the counter from a spool. In front of the counter were two huge barrels; one was filled with pickles in a brine, the other filled with saltine crackers, Mr. Wallace always gave us a cracker to eat while we waited.

Grandpa bought the meat for the family, and always at Pinnus. Both Mr. Wallace's store and Mr. Pinnus' were portions of their homes. Mr. Pinnus' store was further down on Main Street next to the Methodist Church. Steps led down from within his home into the one big room, with a large icebox and a huge round slab of wood like a table. Sawdust covered the floor. I never felt comfortable close to that table with its gigantic knives and spattering of blood. I could envision Grandpa's calves ending their lives on the chopping block, which they did. But not his chickens. Nana wouldn't eat chicken anyhow, so Grandpa's all just died of old age or an occasional mishap with a car. Further down Main Street on Route 25A, at the foot of the hill opposite the old rubber factory, was a group of stores and the post office. One of those stores on that side was Barney Jayne's. The men collected in the back to drink beer and play cards. As children our only interest was the candy counter up front, where, for a penny, we could get a licorice shoestring or two jaw-breakers (Merle's favorite), or a Tootsie Roll. Small businesses came and went. At one time, Tom Lyons had his hardware store where Seaport Deli is today. So did Mr. Meister have his drug store. Rohlston's opened a grocery store managed by Bill Owens – one of God's friendliest souls. He greeted everyone with a smile, knew all of us by name, and loved to tease us. Everyone loved Bill. Years later, we both were in neighboring rooms in the Oncology wing at St. Charles Hospital in Port Jefferson battling cancer with chemotherapy and radiation. Bill lost that battle there. His sweet wife, Gwen, often came in and sat with me.

Mr. Tinker, of Tinker's Point in Setauket, owned a bank on the site of today's Marine Midland Bank. His was a small red brick building. Mr. Dearborn operated this little bank for years. Tinker's estate overlooked Port Jefferson harbor and after his death, an auction was held there. My then sister-in-law Alice Ackerly and I went to it – just for fun I guess. We surely couldn't afford any of the items which were artifacts from around the world. Persians rugs and mahogany statues, jade boxes and exotic crystals.

As children, our social life was very predictable – and very limited. On weekdays we took the bus from Wildfields to school and back. In spring and summer we spent Saturdays playing croquet on the front lawn, jumping rope (Merle had a huge clothesline rope that we could Double Dutch with, roller skating on Pond Path, flying kites, kicking my soccer ball around the yard, reading, playing marbles, listening to the radio, did our chores, played with the dogs and cats, climbed trees, went to the pond, and occasionally went to Port Jefferson or Patchogue or to a birthday party. When Russell Sorensen was visiting Aunt Margaret, he made us butterfly nets and we helped him collect butterflies and moths for his collections. He dropped them into a jar of chloroform and then mounted them with pins on a board.

Every June as Sunday School closed for that season, a picnic was held on Crane Neck on the Eversley Child Estate. We drove down a long pebbled driveway until we reached the cliff above the Long Island Sound. Every family brought its own lunch and spread it out on wooden picnics tables in an open grove. A long path wound down to the beach below. Most went swimming, but Mama never allowed us to do anything but wade in the shallows. We wore our bathing suits made of one-piece wool for this darling event! Then there was Bible school in July.

In winter we skated, shoveled snow, made snowmen and snow forts, rode our sleds from the top of the hill on Pond Path all the way to the intersection of Lower Sheep Pasture and walked to the golf course to go sledding there on our Flexible Flyers. We played ping-pong on the dining room table or Parcheesi or Old Maid on the floor in the hall. We made fridge and molasses taffy which we pulled with buttered hands until it turned a light tan. We wrote poetry, made up plays, sang at the piano when Merle learned to play.

We were completely happy and satisfied with the quiet family life.

On Sundays we went to Sunday school and church and came home to eat roast lamb and listen to the Mormon Tabernacle Choir on the big radio. Nana, who never went to church, was always waiting for the car to pull up at the back door and the three of us to come racing in to join her at the radio. Milton Cross, the announcer, was soon cueing us into the program and we sat silently listening to the beautiful volume and sound of this faraway choir. In the evening, when the opera came on, Daddy would open his bedroom door and close his eyes and listen and sometimes hum the arias.

Sometimes in the summer the posters would go up all over town for the circus. Ringling Brothers was coming! We counted the days! Every time we passed the face of the clown smiling at us, we looked to be sure that the circus was still coming. We asked all our friends in school – every one of them asked, "Are you going to the circus?"

"Sure," they'd all say, but the Chicken Hill kids were never there to see the marvelous magic of the animals, the trapeze artists, the clowns, the band. The tent usually went up in the fields in Port Jefferson Station. The elephants helped lift the poles into place. We sat on wooden benches and the clowns sold us balloons and popcorn. Mom always took us. Sometimes Grandpa went, too.

Sometimes the gypsies came into Setauket, and with them the organ grinder with his little brown monkey, holding out his cup for our pennies, standing on a corner or in front of a store.

"The gypsies are bad people," Nana would tell us. "They steal!"

"What," I wondered, "could this man possibly want to steal?" He had it all: a beautifully painted wagon and a brown monkey.

I wanted so much to hug the little bundle of fur but, of course, Mama wouldn't let us near him. We threw our pennies on the ground and watched him pick them up and listened to the music pour out as the organ grinder cranked the handle. All the best life could ever offer!

"How did you become a gypsy?" I wondered, as he walked away down Route 25A toward Port Jefferson.

Port Jefferson is five miles away and it spelled excitement when we were children. Every summer Mom and Grandpa took us on the Park City Steamship (the original one) to Bridgeport, Connecticut. Mom shopped in a large department store there with us three kids in tow; Grandpa went on his own looking for special items. We children always returned with a toy. Grandpa's Packard was awaiting us on the Port Jefferson dock as the ferry returned. We were weary, happy passengers. The nearest shopping center on land was at Sweezey and Newins in Patchogue. My grandparents shopped there as they did at Kallers in Patchogue, in a store owned and operated by the grandfather of the young man who runs the Setauket store today.

On the Fourth of July, Grandpa hung the big flag on the front porch across the doorway and brought out the sets of little flags that fit on the hood ornament of his car. We all piled in and left for the parade in Port Jefferson – Grandpa, Mom, Merle, Muriel and me. We girls had our individual flags to wave. Grandpa parked near the Presbyterian Church and we stood on the sidewalk waiting. My heart leapt when the first drums could be heard as the parade came down the hill from Port Jefferson Station. Fire engines, sirens screaming, bands, fancy decorated cars, a clown or two – it was the height of fun in the eyes of a child. After the parade, we had a "picnic" lunch at home and then we went with Grandpa to Stony Brook to get two quarts of hand-packed Reid's ice cream from the drug store. After supper we all left for Port Jefferson again to see the fireworks. Sometimes Nana joined us and sat in the car which Grandpa parked on the dock. The fireworks went off a barge anchored in Port Jefferson harbor. As soon as we returned, Uncle Nard and Grandpa set off the fireworks that they had bought at Ottinger's store in Port Jefferson. Personal fireworks were legal then. They had Roman candles and sky rockets and firecrackers. They placed the fireworks in the piles of sand left at the side of the road by the highway department ready for the annual tar-ring. The truck could come through spraying the black ooze across the road and the road crew would follow throwing shovels full of sand on the wet tar, from these piles at roadside. When it dried, the car tires flattened it down and for days we had flecks of tar on our shoes and clothing.

The Fourth of July was an eventful day. From that point on, we were allowed to go in swimming! We had shed our winter underwear, our high top shoes, wore cotton socks with sandals and cotton dresses with sleeveless cotton undershirts beneath our slips. Surely we would not get pneumonia until at least Halloween!

Mom gave us each packages of sparklers to hold and boxes of punk to light them with. We took our twenty-five-cents' allowance to buy whatever else we wanted. Merle and I bought strings of firecrackers which we set off under tin cans that went flipping into the air on Pond Path. Muriel – sweet, quiet, demur little Muriel – always used her money to buy cherry bombs which would have blown her hand off if she hadn't been super-careful! She never could take part with Merle and I in our competition games outside – but, by God, this was one day of triumph when she scared the two of us to death!

Ethel Greenlawn was the daughter of one of Nana's friends when they lived in Floral Park. She was divorced from Basil Greenlawn, a dashing looking businessman with a thick, dark moustache. Ethel would come to visit for weeks at a time, something we girls looked forward to with relish. Ethel was not like the other women we knew in this farming community. Not quite! She was a dyed red-headed dancer who wore short satin dresses and smoked. We were totally spellbound by her. She laughed and joked, and the house bubbled over when she was there.

When Nana died, Ethel Greenlawn arrived for the funeral and stayed for few days. When the minister arrived in the evening for prayers with the family, we three girls were sent to the kitchen to do our homework. Ethel was upstairs, not caring to join in the sad scene in the living room. We heard her moving about upstairs and knew she'd soon be down to make the coffee as she'd said she would.

Mom had bought us girls fancy old rubber aprons with pleated edges in pink and gray. They hung on hooks in the pantry. Next to the stove was a towel rack which swung out across the door leading into the hall. We quickly grabbed a cold rubber apron, hung it on the rack where it filled the doorway, and shut out the kitchen lights. Ethel came bouncing down the stairs, swinging her dancer's legs over the banister as she always did, scooted down the hallway to the kitchen, through the darkened doorway – and screamed! The shriek penetrated the solemn moment like a knife. We, of course, were doubled over with laughter until the adults appeared one by one to chastise us and send us to bed.

The Setauket school was high on a hill overlooking Setauket harbor. It was typical of all schools built on Long Island in the early twentieth century. It resembled a square gray box with a belfry on top and long windows on every side. There was no kindergarten, so we all entered first grade to read and do cursive handwriting at age five for many of us.

We three girls all had Miss Hulse (later Mrs. Heidtman) in first grade; Miss Rodgers in second grade; Mrs. Jones in third grade; Miss Hyde in fourth grade – Miss Hyde was quite a gal. More than once we saw her sitting on the married principal's lap in his office. She wore startling red shoes, tight skirts and lot of bright lipstick. Once she must have had some "physical" problem, for at lunch time she took off her underpants, washed them, and put them on the radiator to dry. The trouble was, she forgot to remove them from there before we kids all returned from recess. The boys had spasms over that one, pointing and guffawing.

By the time I was in fifth grade, Miss Rodgers had become Mrs. James Barnett and had moved up from second grade. She was my favorite so I was happy about that.

In sixth grade, we all had Mrs. Pfeiffer who was very strict and could even scare the tough Chicken Hill boys. Some of them were pretty old for sixth grade, having been "left back" repeatedly. One noon hour, one or more of them sneaked back into the classroom and wherever Mrs. Pfeiffer had written a "W" on the board, they added a penis between the two loops. The girls were either shocked or so naïve that hey had no idea as to what it represented. Most of the boys were scared for the wrath to come. Mrs. Pfeiffer almost had apoplexy!

In seventh grade we had Mrs. Ethel Darling – a very overweight woman who was a whiz at math, one of the few Democrats in Suffolk County, and an avid stamp collector. She had most of us sending away for "stamps on approval."

But the greatest teacher we ever had was Elizabeth Hendrickson – a tall, thin, soft-spoken lady who sincerely cared about us all in eighth grade. If she didn't like the kids we associated with, she subtly changed seats and got us involved with others. By now, some of the boys were as old as sixteen. One girl was pregnant. Some could barely read. Somehow she got them all to come to school and get away from their poverty and abuse in dysfunctional families if only for a few hours. She truly loved us. The majority of us did go on to high school and those who didn't were better off for having been in Mrs. Hendrickson's class.

The bus routes were long by today's standards. Jess Eikov and his brother, Bob, owned and operated the two buses. Jess was funny, friendly and patient. Sometimes our route wound around South Setauket, up to Poulos's where it turned, out to Old Town Road. where it turned at Norwood Avenue and, if one bus was in repairs, we went to Old Field Point to pick up all the kids whose parents worked on the estates there – before climbing the hill to the Setauket High School where we all attended, first grade through twelfth.

Tonight I waited impatiently for sunset. The pink and lavender streaks finally faded away behind the "Old House." It was cold out, near freezing, and I felt chilled as I carefully made my way in the dark along my brick path in the backyard to the field between us and Wildfields. I could see the bright lights in the upstairs hall and bathroom and the kitchen below. The Chinese students moved about unaware of my nearby presence. A March wind rumpled my hair and made me shudder.

Then I looked to the northwest sky and there it was – as clear as if I'd painted it there – the Comet Hale-Bopp; its full tail evident. At age seventy-four I had never seen anything like it! Over one hundred million miles away, and yet my aged, bleary eyes could see it clearly. I came in and got my son Leonard, and we both stood in the cold field and marveled at God's wonder. Two or three hours later, we went out the front door and watched the lunar eclipse taking place in the southern sky. All in one night! April 23, 1997. Palm Sunday, Hosanna!

The television reported cloudy skies in New York City, making visibility poor and the possibility of seeing these things doubtful. But here at Wildfields the sky was clear, cloudless, and the show memorable.

My mom always called her mother "Mama" (as I called mine until I was in my teens). Uncle Nard called his mother "Mother." Mom called her father "Papa," Uncle Nard called him "Father." I always wondered why.

Grandpa never seemed well to me after Nana died. He still had his garden, drove to the post office at the millpond every evening to get his paper and the mail, went to church faithfully, played cards with Percy Smith and friends, attended Royal Arcanum meetings, fed his chickens, milked his beloved "Pet", ate his lunch in Port Jefferson, and listened to the radio. But a great chunk of his heart was gone when his Elsie left us. There had never been and never would be anyone to take her place. Occasionally he would travel to visit relatives or old friends. The Tobiasens, (cousin Edith and cousin Charles) had moved to Middletown, Connecticut, and there was still a residue of Sellecks and friends in or near Middletown, New York. As his heart continued to weaken, he often passed out suddenly – a concern to all of us, especially as he continued to drive.

Grandpa had little money left. He had lost a great deal on the Stock Market. He was "land poor", and sold some of it to G.G. Hunter who then built the houses along Pond Path on the eastern side between the two Sheep Pasture Roads. He sold land in Centereach but he had little income. As kids, we were becoming increasingly aware of these changes but it was the Great Depression years and most of our friends were worse off than we were. It was a rare event when Mom took us to Port Jefferson to the movies (where Theatre Three is now). It cost .10 cents each and on Saturdays you got an item of Depression glass as a bonus incentive to make you return to add to your set. It was called Athena Hall then. Later the Grescoulds took it over and make a machine shop in the basement. Movies were still shown upstairs and it was renamed the Port Jefferson Theatre. Even later, the Brookhaven Theatre opened in Port Jefferson Station and then the large complexes opened all over the area. By then, the theatre had closed and was soon taken over by Theatre Three, a local acting group who gave performances upstairs and down.

Going to Patchogue was like going to Eden. From isolation of Wildfields it seemed like a paradise to our young eyes. Mama always took us three girls to shop at The Bee Hive and Sweezey and Newins as it was called then. As often as needed Mama went to Mrs. Vieteg's to order her corsets (which she wore all her life, until she was too ill to get dressed). It was just that she grew up wearing them and she felt uncomfortable without them. Her newest "best corset" was rolled up and kept in a long box in her dresser in the underwear drawer. The "old corset" she wore about the house. I suppose it would be the same for me if the next generation decided to go bra-less – although I'd have a *much bigger* problem than Mom ever had!

In the Bee Hive Store the money was shipped across the store to the office by some sort of pneumatic device. Change was made and the cylinders shot back to the clerk. It was our greatest fascination. Mom could shop for hours and know that we'd be standing, gawking upward as these metal containers shooting across the ceiling of the store.

Across the street on the corner was Sweezey and Newins. Most of our shopping was done upstairs where the clerks all knew us on sight. Mom kept an account there for as long as she lived on Long Island. She would have loved to have known there was a Sweezey's in Setauket! Wherever she went, wherever she lived, she bought bedspreads and linens and towels. Something about these items gave her special joy. Maybe because they could be used in her room, on he bed, on her body. Nothing else at Wildfields was hers except the furniture in her room and ours. She never had the joy of owning her own home. How did she ever become so strong of spirit when her mother died? When her husband died? She was so brave, so fearful, but so full of courage.

At fifteen I was babysitting on weekends, and in the summer I worked as a waitress at the Stony Brook Prep School for boys ...and falling in love.

"You're in love with love," Mom told me one day when I was swooning over some gawky high school boy. And next it was the movie star, Dick Powell. Typical teenager. Boys were beginning to get driver's licenses and own cars or borrow their Dad's to take girls to movies or to Gramma's in Port Jefferson for ice cream sodas. Cars were spinning into Grandpa's driveway for Merle, Muriel, and me every weekend. All local boys. No one was serious, no one smoked, no one drank, no one ever heard of "uppers " or "downers." Millie Heinz adopted me as her third daughter, realizing that my mother was seldom able to be home as she worked as a live-in domestic. Dad was ill or drunk. Millie's daughter, Marjorie, and I were inseparable. I practically lived at their Bayview Avenue home on weekends. Marge was bright, vivacious, always laughing. She was a leader – like her vivacious mother; and I was a follower – like mine.

We romped through scavenger hunts, dances at the school and neighborhood houses, beach parties, bake sales, shopping sprees, cheerleading, church events, and spent hours and hours of late night talking about boys and clothes and hairdos. One time Marge and I went to Patchogue and bought identical outfits: bright tan shoes (which I thought were ugly), green shirts, blouses with embroidered flowers. We wore them to school the next day and were, of course, the center of attention. A few days later, Marge sold her shoes to another girl because she "didn't like them anymore." I was sure our friendship was over. But I never told Marge how hurt I was. She and her mom had given me a family again. I've never forgotten that.

Merle was close to a beautiful dark-haired, hazel-eyed girl named Leila, who dated all of the most eligible boys in Setauket and in Port Jefferson. They went on to nursing school together as Marge and I went to New Paltz together. When Leila was engaged to marry a doctor, she found herself pregnant with another local boy's baby. She had an abortion and Merle brought her home to Wildfields to recover.

Muriel never made strong single attachments, but had many friends. She and Leila's sister shared a New York apartment and went to dietetic school together. They dated city boys but never got serious with any of them.

We all spent hours talking on the phone as high school kids do today. The phone was a crank phone, fastened to the wall in the hall by the front door and later an upright phone with the ear piece hanging from the side. When we had thunderstorms, blue flashes of light shot from the phone and we were ordered never to go near it. Our listed number was STONY BROOK 38-M.

We were a party line, but seldom heard anyone else conversing on it. Just as we became teenagers, our friends got phones installed in their homes. How convenient! The telephone, cars and jobs for spending money changed our isolated lives forever. A few of my friends still had no indoor plumbing. The high school, high on the hill beyond what is now Setauket Hardware and Mario's, was our gathering point – that and the neighborhood house by the ponds. Inside the high school on the lower floor was the Principal's office, nurse's office, and a tiny teacher's room. Spreading out from either side of these rooms were the grades from first to sixth. Later portable buildings were placed outside on the east between the school and the ball fields. The teachers knew every family from the day the child began school, sometimes before that. There were many Polish and black families from Chicken Hill generally and from Christian Avenue and the outlying farms. Some of the last names were: Iwanicki, Babsky, Streleckis, Motulsky, Kowalsky, Deptola – all hardworking families who sent their children to school. They were almost all well-behaved, polite, generous kids. Scott, Sell, Hart, Thomas, Burns, Cuffee – all families from generations of African American and Indian heritage. The rest of us were WASPS mainly. We were from families who had lived here for nine or ten generations. There were two or three Jewish families.

On the hill, the school was life away from home from the day we arrived with our pencil boxes, new pencils, an eraser and a ruler, a bottle of Carter's ink and straight pens with removable points (later fountain pens were invented), our Laidlaw Readers, geography books, arithmetic books and pads and notebooks – our parents bought our books.

Upstairs, two rooms on the south side could be opened up with sliding doors to provide one big room for the Friday morning assemblies, and Friday night or noon hour dances. After the portable buildings were brought to the site, there was room upstairs for a library and a typing room. A music and art Room was made in the basement as was the science room and lab. Coach Dean Royce, had his desk and locker in the basement hall. The boys' and girls' bathrooms were also in the basement. I remember the time when the toilets were changed to automatic flush toilets, which flushed as soon as you sat down, spraying your buttocks and genitals and terrifying us as young children..

Around Christmas, Roy Tyler, the talented custodian would go from room to room putting his beautiful colored chalk drawings of Santa, reindeer and other Christmas scenes on each blackboard.

When the music department was added, Miss Johnson was hired to teach music and art. During the summer of her first year in Setauket, she began giving instrument lessons and by school's opening she had both band and orchestra organized. We had no way to get to practice to participate, and all three of us were working at Stony Brook anyhow. This was probably some time around 1938. But in September we were all part of the first glee club that Setauket High School had ever heard. Our first performance was on the stage upstairs in the fire house, where all such school activities were held. We sang in unison; harmony was yet to come. Millie Heinz organized a group of mothers who sewed red capes for each of us, parents paying for the material if they possibly could. We were so proud! Tabernacle Choir here we come!

Carolyn Johnson was a remarkable person. Within a year she also had an octet to which Muriel, Merle and I belonged. She took us to places like the P.T.A meetings and the Masonic Lodge in Port Jefferson to sing. Then we went a step further and the glee club put on operettas-all in costume. We learned dances, chorus, solos – all in stride. We never doubted that we could pull if off. Some of the band had uniforms; the orchestra played at school programs. Parents never outwardly lamented the use in school taxes and proudly came to all activities. Well, most parents. Dad never came to any of them. Even though I was aware of his unsociable attitudes, I still thought he just didn't care.

Miss Johnson became Mrs. Boomer soon after I left high school. She was killed in an auto / bus accident on the west coast years later.

Harold Fogg organized the first science fair ever held in Setauket. All of the rooms and hallways on the second floor of high school were filled with displays. All three of us belonged to the science club – a group of high school students that rotated meetings in their respective homes. We did exceptional research for that era in schools. Each had to produce a project and "paper" to be presented at one of the meetings. Flora Frank and I did one in my Junior year (her senior) on brain conditioning and stimuli. Flora who made a fortune in local real estate, still shows an interest in the functions of the brain. Mine is limited to "Why the hell can't I remember that!"

Once Mr. Fogg brought what he said was a stray cat in for an experiment at school. He placed it in a barrel in the science room. We had already dissected frogs and knew what was coming. Several of us girls, went into the lab at lunch time, removed the cat, took it away from the building and set it free. Mr. Fogg was not pleased. He sent three boys out to look for it and unfortunately, they found it. Back in the barrel it went. This time with chloroform added. Within moments the cat was dead and the dissection began. Within her belly were four kittens. I don't believe we *ever* forgave Harold Fogg for so enlightening us. Their tiny pickled bodies, suspended in formaldehyde sat on the lab shelf for as long as I can remember. None of the boys received a *yes* for a date for month.

Mom now had three teenagers to raise. Although Uncle Nard had remarried, lived across the street in the Homestead, had two sons – Dave and Burnell – he never became involved in Merle's life. Once, though, when Merle was going to her senior prom, Aunt Margaret made her prom dress, with Merle's help. It was pink dotted swiss with a tight bodice, very full skirt, and over one hundred buttons down the front. Merle covered every button by hand with the same dress material and sewed each one in place on the garment. It took her weeks to cover these, but how beautiful she looked that night.

After graduating from high school, Merle left Wildfields to go to nursing school at St. John's Hospital in Brooklyn. I missed her greatly. We had had such fun together, playing soccer and softball. She was the girl team's pitcher and *very* good at it.

Evenings were spent around the piano. She taught me duets. We three sang every new song that she learned to play. She had taken piano lessons first from Mr. Jung in Port Jefferson Station, paid for with quarts of milk rich with cream.

When Merle moved to Miami years later, she rented a piano for the season. By the time World War II had started, she had left St. John's Hospital and was working at Mather Hospital in Port Jefferson. There she met Mary Reboli and, since Mary's husband John was away in the service, they both took off for Miami every winter. Once, when I was a patient at Mather for an appendectomy, she called from Miami to wish me well. A long distance phone call was a big deal in those days! I was in agony and she had me get a nurse-friend on the phone and told her what to do to get rid of my pain!

When I was in college at New Paltz, she was still watching over me – telling me not to drink too much beer! "You are too idealistic," she'll tell me. "You trust people too much. You think you can change them! Get into the real world."

I was deep in poetry writing and intellectual thoughts as college seems to foster. Well I soon got into that "real world." World War II saw to that.

Merle and Mary Reboli returned to Long Island every spring and worked at Mather Hospital on the night shift, 7PM to 7AM. Mather was then a two-story brick building facing North Country Road. Merle and Mary ran the entire second floor at night. One end housed all the maternity patients and babies, and the other the women's medical and surgical. Downstairs were men's medical and surgical, pediatrics and the offices next to the wide lobby. The basement held the kitchen, operating room and morgue. A dumbwaiter carried the trays of food up to the patients and nurses on each floor. Each floor had its own linen closet and kitchenette.

On the second floor a gas burner heated formula for the new babies. It sputtered and popped with loud bangs. When I worked with Merle as an aide one summer, it was my job to fix formula. The stove scared me to death. I also had to get our evening midnight meal from the deserted, eerie kitchen next to the morgue – and to help with bed pans, changing babies, feeding babies, patients back rubs and whatever else Merle needed me for. There was a second aide shared by Merle and Mary, a deaf woman named Helda, who usually turned her hearing aide off because she couldn't stand the noise. Merle and Mary took delight in walking behind her saying obscene things which they know she couldn't hear. They were often rough and raucous. One late night, Mary came down the quiet hall. "My ass is so tired, I'm dragging furrows down this hall," she said. All the patients were not sleeping and room by room the infectious laughter spread from one end of the building to the other. Best medicine they ever had.

There was a male resident training to be a nurse. He spoke little English. Merle and Mary trained him in English. The hospital nursing supervisor was a stern "old battle-ax" (quote the two M's who took no nonsense from anyone. They taught the poor man to say: "Would you sleep with me for a big red apple?" They gave him an apple, told him the supervisor would love his gift and sent him off to relay his memorized message. They knew she wouldn't fire them. There was no one else to do their jobs! On some nights part-time nurses came in to help from 7 p.m. to 11 p.m. to prepare patients for night and help with the babies. One of these was Kathleen Hauser. She and Merle became very close friends. When Merle was married and living in Miami, Florida, Hauser and her husband moved close by. Hauser believed she had cancer and one night a frantic call from her husband sent Merle racing to their home. Hauser was dead. "I'm sure that she committed suicide," Merle told me. All the clothes were washed, ironed and neatly laid out or in place in drawers, her husband's (I think his name was Joe) clothes laid out for the next day: socks, underwear, shirt on the dresser top. Her bank accounts and legal papers laid out on the dresser next to his clothes. What a loss. Hauser was such a good nurse and intelligent, devoted wife and friend. Perhaps as a nurse, she had seen and knew too much. The rate of any cancer cure was extremely low then. Whether she actually had cancer or not, we never knew. Merle often said that nurses, herself included, were the worst of all patients because they knew all the possibilities. But Merle was the best of nurses. One of my friends said she planned her pregnancies around Merle's return from Florida each spring. She'd have no other nurse in her delivery. Her scientific mind gave her logic; her intelligence gave her answers; her determination to succeed in spite of rejection gave her courage; her love of God gave her compassion.

In June of 1937, news in Stony Brook came onto the front page of the New York Times newspaper.

In 1925, Alice McDonnell, heiress to a sizable fortune, married William H. Parsons, whose family made millions in Standard Oil. For a while the couple lived in New York City, but in 1929 they moved permanently to their 11-acre estate, Long Meadow Farms, located in Stony Brook, Long Island. The Parsons had a rather unusual hobby: they raised plump, "well-bred" chickens for the fancy restaurant trade. By all accounts, the two of them enjoyed their quiet life.

In 1931, Alice became ill and needed someone as a companion / housekeeper. On the recommendation of her sister, Alice hired Anna Kuprianova – an attractive Russian immigrant who spoke little English. She was very competent and when Alice recovered from her illness, Anna stayed on as the Parsons' housekeeper.

Oddly enough, Anna owned a valuable recipe for squab paste used on canapés. Together she and the Parsons formed a partnership of sorts. The Parsons quit raising chickens and began raising squabs to use in the squab paste. Before long, no party was considered a success unless Parsons-Kuprianova squab paste canapés were served.

It appeared that everything was fine in the Parsons household. When Anna's five-year-old son, Roy, came to live at Long Meadow Farms, the Parsons treated him like their own child. They had no children due to an accident Alice had in her youth. Before long, Roy Kuprianova became known as Roy Parsons and in 1936, when Anna took out citizenship papers, she changed her name to Anna Kuprianova-Parsons.

Early in the morning of June 9, 1937, Alice drove her husband to the station to catch a commuter train to New York City, then returned home. At 11:00 a.m. that morning, a black sedan occupied by a middle-aged couple pulled up to the house. After speaking with them for a few minutes, Alice called out to Anna, who was working in the kitchen, saying she was riding with the couple to look at a nearby estate she was trying to rent out. Alice Parsons climbed in the car, and was never seen again.

When Mr. Parsons arrived home around 7 p.m., Anna told him his wife had been gone most of the day and had not returned. Mr. Parsons conducted a quick search of the property, then called the police.

When the police arrived, they began a search of the estate, including the Parsons' car parked in front of the house. Nothing was found in the car, so it was locked up and the search continued. At 1:30 the following morning, a policeman happened to shine his flashlight in the car and noticed a note stuck under the floorboard in the back seat. It was a ransom note demanding $25,000 within twenty-four hours!

William Parsons and Anna Kuprianova-Parsons, joined by Alice's two brothers, waited at Long Meadow Farms for word from the kidnappers, but no contact was made. Mr. Parsons offered a reward for his wife's return, but no one came forward with any information. Eventually the FBI were called in. After a few months of investigation, the FBI turned the case back over to the local authorities, claiming Mrs. Parsons was murdered, not kidnapped. Local detectives relentlessly searched the property from one end to the other again, but found nothing. One of the detectives was Alvin Smith, a close friend of Uncle Nard's and Aunt Margarite's. A few years ago Alvin let Leonard go through his notebooks on the Parsons case.

As the days stretched out and the search proved fruitless, the excitement in the local area continued. Blood hounds were brought in to search the surrounding woods. Muriel and I listened to their baying as they searched between the "Old House" and Stony Brook – an area which was all woodland then. While we were listening to the hounds proclaiming their worth, my small radio in our bedroom announced that a phone call had been received anonymously at Dare's drug store in Port Jefferson demanding ransom money for Mrs. Parsons. It was a strange, frightening feeling. We were sitting at Wildfields between the locations of whomever phoned and the bloodhounds!

The Parsons case was never solved. Mrs. Kuprianova and her son moved to California a short time later. So did Mr. Parsons, and speculation following their marriage there was inevitably suspicions. Over the years, their son has been questioned, a graveyard in Stony Brook has been partially dug up following reports by an eighty-year-old man who believes she may be buried there in the black cemetery because of a mysterious grave that appeared soon after the murder. It was stopped by an Indian declaring that they were digging on sacred ground. It would have been much simpler just to have taken her body out into the Long Island Sound any night in the many miles of isolated areas back then.

The excitement lasted for a long time. Newspapers carried stories for months. The radio news brought out each new lead, new fact. Even today, papers pick up on the story of the unsolved mystery of the disappearance of Alice Parsons.

The Long Island winds woke me up at 5 a.m. screeching, moaning and banging things about as a front moved across. Several friends have called to say they have no electricity. Here we seldom have twisters, although I have seen them whirling across the potato fields out east. But we do have hurricanes! The most recent very damaging one was Gloria in September of 1985. When Gloria approached the Island, the tallest trees began swaying. I went "down street" into King Kullen for cat food and milk. A steady thin stinging rain was coming down. Schools were already closed in anticipation of the storm which was churning up the Atlantic Coast headed straight for Long Island.

I hurried home to recheck kerosene lamps and flashlights and get a big pot of coffee made and poured into thermos jugs. I first stopped at Wildfields to get Aunt Margaret. Two days before, I had taken her for cataract surgery at St. Charles Hospital in Port Jefferson, and the day before to the eye surgeon who said all was well but I didn't want her left alone during the storm.

"Oh I'll be all right," she'd explain. "I can see fine now."

But as we talked on the side porch the wind pace quickened rapidly and she changed her mind. We carried in all porch items: chairs, a folded metal table Vic had left there for parties, plants and a source pot for watering them. When we arrived at Stony Brook the rain was pelting us and wind gusts were bending huge branches. I immediately went to the stove to heat water for coffee. And then the electricity went off! No coffee! I would have to brave the worse storm to hit Long Island since the 1938 Hurricane cold turkey!

The damage was extensive everywhere around us. The trunks of our backyard maples moved in their sockets. The storm crossed the island at the town of Islip and we were exactly in the "eye." As the winds stopped, I went outside to see if a downed huge front yard maple had damaged the house. The phone rang and Leonard told Jim Clancy, who was east of us in Rocky Point and not in the "eye" yet, that I was outside. "What in hell ails her!?" he yelled. "She'll be killed!"

I was instead much alive and looking up at a totally quiet blue sky, but moments later the backside of the hurricane hit and I scurried inside.

We had *no* warning of the 1938 Hurricane. In fact, Muriel and I went to school on Jess Eikon's bus as usual. By mid-afternoon, the storm was hitting full-force. Classes came to a halt while school staff and officials tried to figure out how to get us home. Most of us were in the upstairs rooms with windows facing west and north. We could see pieces of the roof and bricks flying from the old factory at the top of Chicken Hill. Those who lived there were sent home scattering like leaves in a fall wind as they raced for shelter, big brothers and sisters clutching little children. No one from the school that I know of escorted the kids to Chicken Hill. But on the Route 25A side by the harbor, a human chain of parents and neighbors, mostly men, was forming. The school, sitting on top of the hill overlooking Setauket Harbor, had a long row of wide steps from the front door to the street below. A group of tall pines clustered neatly at the bottom of the hill. One by one, or two or three together, the children led by the custodian, principal and male teachers, were delivered to parents waiting below; to the human chain along the non-wild harbor and to home.

But how would they get us home to Nassakeag and Old Field? Because of our exposure on the hilltop, the staff felt that they must get us out. We weren't afraid; just excited. Two of the biggest high school boys were sent down the hill to Gnarled Hollow Road to see if the buses could get out that way. Jess and Bob had already gotten the buses to the school parking lot and thought that Gnarled Hollow Rd. would be the safest route to Nassakeag. But the boys returned to say that the creek had completely flooded the road! It was decided to send buses out to Route 25A and the Old Field children would go in various teachers' cars. Winds at times were over 200 mph! One of the teachers was our favorite Peg Lowry West, who is Ben Tyler's mother-in-law. She was assigned to take children to Old Field and as she made her last delivery, an official told her to, "Get out of here fast. This is the last road open!" So she tells in Ben Tyler's article in the Three Village Herald on the 1938 Hurricane. Branches snapped about us, sparks flew from downed wires. Rain blinded the view but we crept along. When we finally got to the St. George's Golf Course on Sheep Pasture Road and the Matusky farm, Jess got out and looked up Pond Path. The Matusky boys helped move downed trees off the road before we could get up the hill. We were met by obviously anxious relatives; soaked just by running up the driveway to Wildfields, but holding onto an unforgettable memory.

It didn't end there. The next day we took the bus as usual. No electricity in school didn't seem to phase anyone. In fact, it was almost two weeks before it was restored. We had a few minor detours in route. Kids from the harbor area told of boats on lawns, much flooding making the roads around the harbor impossible. Our pump stopped of course. There was no "city water" then. We had our own well over at the "Old House" and the pump-house was still outside the kitchen door. For days, Grandpa had to drive up to Tommy Hawkins where they pumped precious water by hand into large milk cans and bought it back to Wildfields.

As Muriel and I got off the bus the day after the storm two of the high school boys met us and eventually six of us piled into one of their cars and headed east to the Hamptons, spurred on by radio reports of the unbelievable damage there. The reports were not over-estimated. It was shocking! Beautiful homes along the Great South Bay and along the Atlantic Ocean were totally demolished or washed out to sea. The streets were left with those great old trees criss-crossing them like Lincoln Logs. Few roads along the shore were even passable. We were not allowed near the water's edge. We ate our bag lunches in the car and headed back to school in time to get our busses at dismissal. We didn't count on Mr. Welch, the principal, to be waiting for us, not a bit happy or understanding about our needs for discovery. Our parents had already been notified of our truancy.

Muriel

At Smith's Point I see you
Swinging in the winter wind,
Hair flying – snow blowing
Against your cheeks.
You were like a new child
Full of all the joy of life.
The ocean beat like a
Giant's heart behind you;
The reeds bending,
The swing creaking
And your laughter
Haunting my mind.

Ruth Rothermel

How close Muriel and I became as we grew older! It no longer mattered that she was more frail than I. We no longer needed to play soccer. She could sew beautifully; I couldn't sew a stitch. She was a masterful cook and gardener. When Mom left home to work in doctors homes or care for some elderly person, Muriel took over. She had a dog, part collie-part German shepherd, named Laddie who was her companion. He got her away from her books and out into the fresh air. We would watch the mail plane fly over each evening and the pilot would tip his wings as we waved to him. We spent our .25 cent weekly allowance on jigsaw puzzles which we shared. Daddy brought home the galleys from the Daily News comic strips which a friend in Rocky Point gave him. We sprawled across his bed every evening reading them. The kids at school couldn't figure out how we knew what was happening to Dick Tracy before they read it in the paper. Sometimes we had galleys for a whole week ahead.

Dad had several friends in Rocky Point. One was a marathon swimmer named Paul Brunner who taught us all how to swim at the little strip of sand at the end of Beach Street in Port Jefferson. Mom thought the water was contaminated (and it probably was in Port Harbor) but let us go. Within two weeks we were floating, treading water, doing the American crawl and the breast stroke. Another man, whose name I've forgotten, was drawing up plans for a bridge to Connecticut. He often came and spent the day with Aunt Margaret. How she knew him I don't think I ever knew. He was brilliant, and very eccentric. Many have followed his dream of a bridge, but it obviously has never materialized.

In 1939 we all went to the Worlds Fair. The Long Island Rail Road put a special stop at the fair's gates and we went in as class groups to see the famous Trylon and Perisphere and the hundreds of great exhibits – I remember feeling sad that the Czech exhibit was only half-built and couldn't open. Little did we know that we were just a blink away from WWII. Life was just full of wonderment. We had heard radio broadcasts from Admiral Byrd's camp at the North Pole, had seen suits that his men wore made of a new wonder material called nylon. We began wearing nylon stockings. They dried unbelievably fast! When the war did come and nylon was used for parachutes among other things, we couldn't buy nylon hosiery (except on the black market) so we painted our legs with a brown liquid.

When WWII broke out, I was in college. Muriel had left New Paltz and gone home. She worked in a private home for awhile and then she and Mom got jobs in Grumman and Republic Aircraft factories making parts for the military planes that would soon be in "dog-fights" with the enemy or flying over the South Pacific. Women began to wear pants-slacks, which were safer to wear around machinery. They wore bandanas on their heads which identified the plant that they worked in; heavy shoes and socks on their feet.

They carried lunch boxes just as the men did. Mom, at 4' 11", had difficulty reaching the parts of the aircraft and was removed to the section of the assembly line where she put small parts together. Muriel climbed ladders into the fuselage or against the wings. Once she received a concussion when she turned into an outstretched pipe. Gas and meat were rationed but as aircraft employees they seemed to be assured that they would get to work. Once they moved to an apartment in Hicksville, they took buses to plants, saving their ration stamps for trips to Wildfield's. Meat was such a luxury that we saved stamps for weeks, just to get a pot roast! The bulk of meat went to bases abroad and Navy ships at sea. We became brilliant at ways to get to the beaches since they were patrolled and cars could not be used for recreation. We gave up West Meadow for isolated areas and often walked miles to get to the water.

We donated blood as often as possible. Muriel was occasionally turned down due to her weight. One had to weigh at least 100 and she normally was around 98 pounds.

Grandpa was an air raid warden and patrolled Pond Path, lower and upper Sheep Pasture Roads and surrounding areas. He went out every night looking for lights. We all had "black out" shades which had to be lowered at night. Offenders were fined. One time at New Paltz my teaching supervisor asked me to sit with her on night patrol. We climbed a Forest Ranger tower and reported every small plane sighted – often just a dot of light moving far away in the dark night. It was a lovely but eerie place atop the Shawangunk Mountains, but I could see why my supervisor didn't want to be there alone.

We knitted scarves and gloves and socks for the servicemen in drab olive-colored wool supplied by the Red Cross and we rolled bandages and collected milkweed for parachutes. Gum wrappers were saved for the foil. We wrote to servicemen all over the world on special air mail paper. We went to USO dances and put on shows for servicemen who came in from Stuart Air Force Base, and we prayed that we wouldn't hear of one more friends "killed in action."

With war on two fronts – Europe and Asia – men left New Paltz State Teachers College one by one – drafted or to join up in a branch of the service. Uniforms were everywhere. As females, we were definitely impressed. As men left jobs to go into the service, women took their places. Muriel eventually went to dietetic school in New York City, and then to work in hospitals on Long Island and in Suffern, New York. At the time of Dad's death, she bought a sailor home with her if we had no *steady*. We dated guys on leave, guys from air bases nearby, guys who were 4F and disqualified for the draft, or just went out as a bunch of girls and danced to jukebox tunes. Many girls became engaged just before their men went overseas. Many tears were shed when weeks went by without hearing from their men. Gold stars appeared in windows; mothers lost sons; daughters lost lovers or husbands. It was so difficult separating from childhood to adulthood and having to face so much death so fast ...so often. We were totally unprepared and so afraid. Where on earth was this loving God that Miss Bessie had taught us to believe in?

On almost every vacation from college, I returned to Wildfields and worked in the summers to earn money so that I could return to college in the fall. The $1 a day that I made at Stony Brook Prep and the $2 or $3 a night working at Gregson's on weekends was all I had. It was at Gregson's that I met Nelson Ackerly, whom I married in 1943. Nelson was good-looking – a rough cut face, tall and thin with brown wavy hair and hazel eyes. He and Richie Redding came into Gregson's every weekend until Nelson went into the Navy Air Force. Richie's brother, Winard, was in my class at New Paltz. Both Nels and Richie made good money working as machinists in the defense plants, money which they freely spent. Nel's father had owned a liquor store in Port Jefferson and Nels, his brother Robert and sister Ruth lived with their parents on Vineyard Place in Port Jefferson just behind what is now Scented Cottage Gardens. Another brother, LeRoy, married Alice Smith and they lived with their three children in Mount Sinai, N.Y. Blanche Overton Ackerly (Mom Ackerly to me) kept an immaculate home. She was a darling, tiny, energetic woman – warm and friendly and I loved her dearly. Nel's father, George Ackerly, came down hard on his kids. They could do little to please him, especially when it came to racing his scooter boats on the ice of Great South Bay. The scooters were indigenous to that one area. Unlike the ice boats which also raced on the bay, they had double-runner blades below their beautifully polished wooden hulls. George Ackerly and the other members of the South Bay Scooter Club were a tight-knit group. They raced for blood! They cursed, drank heavily, and spent winter nights following the races drinking and arguing over the folly or greatness of their achievements in water race. George wasn't an alcoholic as his three sons became, and he never allowed those sons to take liquor from his store, but he had his wild sprees. The boys obeyed him without question.

George Ackerly, "Pop" as we called him, entered the service in 1942 voluntarily and was a chief petty officer in the U.S. Navy. He was sent almost immediately to North Africa where among other things, he contracted malaria. In the summer of 1943, he returned home a very ill man. He had lost so much weight that his uniform trousers were pinned together. He was medically discharged and returned to pick up his life. It wasn't long before George and his buddies were up to their usual nonsense of never-grow-up-time. More than once the liquor store was "temporarily closed" while Pop, Charlie Koutrackis and Roy Davis had an egg fight on the Main Street of Port Jefferson. Nelson was also a buddy of Roy's but in other places such as Teddy's Bar in lower Port Jefferson or Bill Jacob's Wagon Wheel in Port Jefferson Station.

When Nels wasn't working or drinking, he was out in the harbor on a sailboat or on Fire Island at the family cottage – fishing, clamming, eeling, catching soft shell crabs. After we became engaged, I went with him. By then, the Ackerly's owned two cottages on Fire Island. Life at Wildfields suddenly seemed dull.

Soon after I returned to New Paltz State Teachers College for my senior year, I broke the engagement to Nels because of the warning signals I began to see in regard to his drinking. In October, Marge Heinz and I returned for a three-day Columbus Day weekend. No one but Grandpa was at Wildfields. Dad had died; Mom was working away from home. Millie Heinz urged me to stay with them. Nelson met us at the train and we all went to Arata's in Port Jefferson Station to meet Alice and Roy Ackerly and to bowl. Around midnight we left for Heinz's. Marge went on her own, I told Nelson that I was breaking the engagement and I gave him back the ring. In anger, he threw it out of the car window into thousands of newly fallen leaves. The next morning he returned to fruitlessly search the Heinz's front yard inch by inch. The ring was never found as far as I know, at any rate *he* never found it.

Soon after this, Nels enlisted in the Navy Air Force and trained to fly the Grumman fighter planes used in WWII – first Wildcats, than Hellcats. By spring my whole life changed. Within a few months I'd be out of the college cocoon and into the real world and teaching students. I had signed a contract at Roeliff Jansen Central School District in Hillsdale, N.Y. My salary: $1450 a year.

Marge Heinz had gone to summer school, taking some extra courses and was already teaching there. We picked up where we had left off – from first grade through high school, through all of college, and now entering into our own career as teachers in the same school! We were roommates once again; this time in Mrs. Porteus Boarding House. Along with four or five other teachers from Roeliff Jansen. Mr. Porteus ran a jam-packed county store in Hillsdale, selling mostly hardware. For those of us who were engaged or had boyfriends, they were all far, far away at war or training for battle. The biggest events of our lives were the round-robin basketball tournaments, trips to Great Barrington, Massachusetts or bridge games. We smoked at home but it wasn't allowed at school. We all wrote countless letters.

At Christmas I went home for my vacation. Puricks were giving Marge a bridal shower. Several of my college friends stayed at Wildfields with me as they had to travel a distance to get to the shower. In the middle of the night I was in agony and the next morning Dr. McGalvery came to the house (doctors often made house-calls then), put me in his car and took me to Mather Hospital where he removed my *about to burst* appendix. I recuperated at Millie Heinz's and one day Nelson, in uniform, arrived there with a beautiful satin flowered robe for me. I hadn't seen him for months. We talked and I was aware of a difference in attitude.

"You've changed," I told him.

"The Navy changed me," he replied." "Flying keeps me sober. I don't even want a drink."

When I left Millie Heinz's, I didn't go right back to school although I was already several weeks late. (Doctors didn't get you on your feet until you were healed in those days). On February 4, 1945, in a raging blizzard, I was married to Nelson in his family's living room. Alice and Roy brought the minister with them. Mom came from Setauket. Muriel and a friend came by train from Suffern, N.Y. where they worked and drove Mom there. We got as far as Bay Shore on our honeymoon. The storm continued for the rest of our lives together!

By the end of the school year in 1945, I joined Nelson in Miami where we shared an apartment with Merle after Mary Reboli returned north, to be with her husband, John, who was home either on leave or discharged. William Nelson Ackerly was a Navy fighter pilot stationed at Opa-Locka, a Navy

Base just south of Miami. At first it was exciting. I'd never been in the sub-tropics before. Here were palm trees, pelicans, flamingos, blue-green waters on the coral reefs and great white clouds hanging close to earth moved by the trade winds. It was like a movie-world to me. Merle's apartment was the bottom floor of a stucco building consisting of two bedrooms, a living room, and a fairly large kitchen with an eating area. I soon realized what a poor, untrained housekeeper I was! Nelson, used to his mother's immaculate home and excellent cooking wanted closets cleaned and food prepared as *he* liked it. Most of the kitchen closets held utensils that Merle and Mary never used and abounded in giant cockroaches (called Palmetto bugs by native Floridians), ants and spiders.

Stirred up by my moving things out to clean, giant spiders crawled out and across the ceilings at night. They looked just like tarantulas but I was told that they weren't and were not poisonous. News that there were deadly coral snakes about and painfully poisonous scorpions just made me more miserable!

Merle worked days and on her day off she liked to take the bus down-town to the library or shopping, or go to the waterfront parks or museums. Nelson informed me that I was not to go with her "looking for men." He expected me to be home at whatever hour he arrived. His training and stress intensified as he prepared for carrier landings at sea. With the stress came the drinking again. The ever closer possibility of going into War forever loomed over us. He had no patience. Any excuse sent him out to drink, leaving me alone; expecting me there upon his return. My college education was a threat to his ego. He wanted me to have no contact with old friends. If I wrote to Mom or Muriel, he'd take the letters from the mailbox and open and read them, censoring them before I was "allowed" to send them. We were never a part of the "crowd" at Base. That was too threatening. I might look at someone else. His routine kept him busy and predictable until word came from Warm Springs, Georgia on April 12, 1945 that the President, Franklin D. Roosevelt, had died. All was chaos. Nelson left immediately for the base which, like all others, was put on high alert. We were at war and our leader had left us.

Within hours, Harry S. Truman took his place in history.

In May, Nels was given a two week leave and was to report to an air base near Atlantic City following the leave. We all packed feverishly. Merle had to get her piano returned to the rented store (not an easy feat since trucks were at a premium). We loaded our possessions in and atop of our small red Chevy and headed north. By the time we had reached Georgia, we had to buy three black-market tires, which was at the time all you could get and each one lasting only a few hundred miles. People just took advantage of servicemen who had to move their families from one place to another and sold what they would never begin to pass inspection for "good tires" at outrageous prices. Once we were followed by obvious bandits in a long, isolated stretch. We found a motel and took turns sleeping and watching the car from the window. Before we reached Long Island we had bought five tires. With all the misery of that trip, I was still awed by the beauty of this country. Cities loomed before us in the distance. Merle recited a poem she learned in grade school.

Barbara Frietchie
by John Greenleaf Whittier

Up from the meadows rich with corn,
Clear in the September morn,

The clustered spires of Frederick stand,
Green-walled by the hills of Maryland.

Round about them orchards sweep,
Apple and peach tree fruited deep,

Fair as the garden of the Lord
To the eyes of the famished rebel horde;

On that pleasant morn of the early fall
When Lee marched over the mountain wall,-

Over the mountains winding down,
Horse and foot, into Frederick town.

Forty flags with their silver stars,

Forty flags with their crimson bars,

Flapped in the morning wind: the sun
Of noon looked down, and saw not one.

Up rose old Barbara Frietchie then,
Bowed with her fourscore years and ten;

Bravest of all in Frederick town,
She took up the flag the men hauled down;

In her attic window the staff she set,
To show that one heart was loyal yet.

Up the street came the rebel tread,
Stonewall Jackson riding ahead.

Under his slouched hat left and right
He glanced: the old flag met his sight.

"Halt!"- the dust-brown ranks stood fast;
"Fire!" - out blazed the rifle-blast.

It shivered the window, pane and sash;
It rent the banner with seam and gash.

Quick, as it fell from the broken staff
Dame Barbara snatched the silken scarf;

She leaned far out on the window-sill,
And shook it forth with a royal will.

"Shoot, if you must, this old gray head,
But spare your country's flag," she said.

A shade of sadness, a blush of shame,
Over the face of the leader came;

The nobler nature within him stirred
To life at that woman's deed and word;

"Who touches a hair of yon gray head
Dies like a dog! March on!" he said.

All day long that free flag tost
Over the heads of the rebel host.

Ever its torn folds rose and fell
On the loyal winds that loved it well;

And through the hill-gaps sunset light
Shone over it with a warm good-night.

Barbara Frietchie's work is o'er,
And the Rebel rides on his raids no more.

Honor to her! and let a tear
Fall, for her sake, on Stonewall's bier.

Over Barbara Frietchie's grave,
Flag of Freedom and Union, wave!

Peace and order and beauty draw
Round thy symbol of light and law;

And ever the stars look down
On thy stars below in Frederick town!

When the two weeks were almost up, Nelson and I left for Atlantic City. It was difficult finding a place to live. At nightfall we pulled into a cluster of cabins: "Schooleys" – Major Schooley had been a pilot in WWII and took an immediate liking to Nels. He was quite a bit older than his wife, Molly. Major loved his scotch and let it get out of hand quite often, but he loved to tell stories of his barn-storming days. Molly took me under her wing and I helped her clean cabins each day and she fed us in what had once been a restaurant on the property. They raised rabbits for food (meat was rationed) and sold the pelts for gloves.

Our cabin was one room with a bath. It had a stove, desk, chair, bed, dresser and small closet. Nelson relaxed, kidded Molly and helped Major down his scotch. There were water fights and laughter. Nelson took over assigning cabins in the evening if Major got drunk. It was my introduction to the "One Night Stand" as politicians, Army and Navy personnel, people of all economic status, come and went with their early afternoon "dates." There were "regulars" who left a trail of condoms on the floor and sometimes articles of intimate clothing. Molly and I scrubbed, swept and disinfected. This world was a pigsty needing continuous cleaning but we just laughed about it. The "combinations" were so funny. One man brought his mother and set her up in the next cabin with a bottle. A few hours later all three would leave quite drunk.

We shared our ration stamps for the little meat allowed. Nels ate a big meal at the base and in *those days* I ate very little. In all the months that we lived at Schooleys, Nelson took me out once. We went to Atlantic City to a big Squadron party at one the largest hotels. Life was becoming unbearably lonesome. Even Molly and I ran out of things to laugh about. Once Muriel came to visit me staying for a few days. The war went on; Nelson was oblivious to anyone's needs but his own – typical of all alcoholics, he found excuses to start arguments – to be away to drink. That fall his orders came through to transfer to Quincy, Massachusetts. I hated to leave Schooley's but was also glad to be going away. I had become very depressed. Even Major said, "Leave him. He isn't going to change. I *know!*"

Our little red car headed north to Long Island once more. We picked up winter clothes and visited family before going to Massachusetts. I had never been north along the Atlantic seaboard before. It's rugged beauty captivated me. Route 1 took us into old New England towns, some at the ocean's edge. After checking into a Boston hotel, Nelson left for the Base. He obtained a list of places with rooms to rent and immediately eliminated any with other personnel living there. God forbid I have a friend. He settled on a room in Mrs. Squibb's private home. We had kitchen privileges. The market was several blocks away – within walking distance but hard to carry heavy bags of groceries from. There was a small beach at the end of our street, but I was too shy to go there alone and Nelson refused to give me any money even if I'd wanted to buy a bathing suit. I began a real withdrawal from the world. By now Nelson had molded me from a self-assured intelligent person to a meek, afraid-to-open-my-mouth individual who had no way to escape: no money, no job ...only fear. My back ached. I couldn't eat without nausea. Nelson spent evenings at the Officer's Club without me. The pilots were a reckless bunch, flying their one-seater fighter planes at reckless speeds – under the Cape Cod bridges, just above the ocean waves. It was a game, one that killed the nicest one in the squadron. I wanted to get away from all this horror – but I couldn't. I was pregnant.

On August 6th, 1945 U.S. planes bombed Hiroshima and the War was over. Nelson was transferred to Virginia Beach, Va. to Oceana Naval Air Station. We left Quincy after our afternoon squadron party – that Nels attended – and headed South in our little red car.

We swung onto the New England Turnpike, headed for Long Island. As we reached the first toll booth, we inadvertently hit the gate. Nelson just backed up, threw the money in, and went on. Moments later a state trooper pulled us over. He saw the beer bottles; some empty, some full. He saw the botched attempt by Nelson to remove his license from his wallet. He heard the slurred speech, saw the half-closed eyes, and he saw the Navy officer's uniform.

"Why don't you pull over and sleep," he suggested and let us go.

"Maybe I will die," I thought, "...and this nightmare will end!"

The next day we stopped at Schooley's where I stayed while Nelson went on to Virginia to find living quarters. As we came to their cabins we could hear a scraping sound in the little red car's wheel. Upon inspection, Nels found the lugs had almost worn through the wheel base. Another few miles and the wheel would have flown off!

Mollie and I sat around and talked. She commented that nothing ever changed our men and their selfish drinking. She and Major had the cabins up for sale and were moving to Florida to start a co-op. I never heard from them again.

For awhile we actually shared an apartment complex with two other couples. We rotated use of the kitchen. The Norfolk area was filled with Navy personnel. It was perhaps the largest Naval Base in the country. We were at Virginia Beach a short distance away. Just before Christmas we moved into our own apartment to have room for the baby. We left our trunk, suitcases and clothes there before going on leave to Long Island. We stayed at Mom and Pop Ackerly's. On Christmas Eve Day, Nelson dropped me off at Wildfields to visit Mom, Grandpa, Aunt Margaret. Uncle Nard, Dave and Burnell. Nelson went on to "run errands." After I talked with Grandpa for awhile, waiting for Mom to come home from work; he needed to take his nap so I walked over to visit Aunt Margaret at the "Old House." Suddenly, Grandpa appeared at the door, "Ruth," he called. "Nelson is in Mather Hospital. I'm to take you there."

Nelson, had left Wildfields and headed for the Wagon Wheel where he had drank the afternoon away. Knowing he was drunk, he left his wallet with Bill Jacobs, the owner, and with a few dollars in his pocket headed for Patchogue to visit his friends there. Snow covered the ground and in some places narrowed the road considerably. As Nelson came around the corner on Route 112 in Coram, he met someone coming at him. The man was a Good Samaritan, collecting toys and gifts for the children at St. Charles Hospital in Port Jefferson. The car struck him head on. The Good Samaritan's lungs were both punctured and he died a few hours later.

When I arrived at the hospital one of Pop Ackerly's friends, a local policemen, sat at Nelson's bedside. No one else was allowed to question him.

There was a trial at the Riverhead courts. Nelson appeared with a broken arm and facial cuts and was acquitted of manslaughter charges. Many bottles of his best liquor went with Pop to the trial. He bragged about his political clout.

Now Nelson could not fly. He was summarily discharged from the Navy Air Force. The Navy packed and shipped over his belongings from Virginia Beach, to the Ackerly's home. We had no car. Nelson drank his way through the next five months.

On May 15, 1946 the baby was born. Dr. Werk delivered my beautiful rosy-cheeked girl with a mop of jet black hair after thirty-six hours of hard labor. We made arrangements with Grandpa to rent what had been Merle's room and the sunporch, and Carol came home with me to live at Wildfields.

As Nel's arm healed, he bought an old second-hand car and found odd jobs including painting Wildfields. Eventually he worked at Greswolds Machine Shop again. He, his brother Roy and Uncle Alfred, built row boats in Roy's cellar at night. Roy set up a fishing station at Mount Sinai harbor, rented out the boats and sold bait. His wife, Alice, daughter Jeanne, Carol and I spent many days there while Roy was at work at RCA in Rocky Point. Roy, Nelson and some friends had built Roy's home in Mount. Sinai – a small cape with a big friendly fireplace. Alice raised chickens, geese and a pig or two. All of the Ackerly men were hunters. Before Carol turned five she could tack a sailboat back and forth across Port Jefferson Harbor. Nelson spent a great deal of his free time at the harbor – either at bars or at the Yacht Club on Beach Street, where he and his friend Bill Weit were soon running the water taxi.

We moved into a small apartment in Port Jefferson where the Printer's Devil Restaurant is now located. For awhile Nelson worked for Bud Lundgren in his machine shop next door. As Bill Weit and Nelson became well known around the harbor, they built up a business of repairing boats and boat engines. Nelson's drinking increased to the point that people unknown to me were calling to tell me that he needed help. One was a doctor who said that he knew that Nels was hiding bottles in the oven of the Yacht Club and would give him free medical attention with a new drug if I could get him to his home in Stony Brook.

Nelson would not go. That year he tried to commit suicide.

Business was booming at the harbor – Nels and Bill opened a Marine Supply Store on West Broadway where a bakery is now located. His sister, Ruthie, ran the store. I took a teaching job in Port Jefferson Station and we bought a home on Hawkins Hill in Stony Brook. We *seemed* to have everything any young couple could want. Surely he'd get the self-esteem he needed and stop his excessive drinking. I was close to his family. They gave me such support knowing he was drowning in his fight with the addiction. There were affairs with young girls and one-night stands. One time he brought home crab-lice from a Port Jefferson brothel.

He repaired boat engines perfectly and never remembered doing them. He once came home drunk and parked in the patio instead of the driveway. I was so ashamed to face the neighbors. He would agree to go to Alcoholics Anonymous; go to one meeting and then "didn't need that." "Wasn't one of them." He and Bill took in two other partners in their now incorporated business. One was Jim Davidson, agent for President Truman's daughter Margaret, for the Firestone Music Hour on radio and The Robert Shaw Chorale among others. Jim's connection with the Firestone Company opened the door for a second business venture and the four men started a Firestone retreading plant in the large building next door to the Marine Supply Store. Later, the Port Jefferson Town Hall was built there. The war had ended but the supply of new tires was still negligible. The possibility of a thriving retread business was definite.

But Nelson was becoming frequently violent. Several times I left him for the security of Wildfields. He joined Alcoholics Anonymous repeatedly, but never stayed with it long enough to help. They were really there for him. Sometimes, they came to our home and sat with him throughout the night. In the morning he'd go with them to a meeting. Occasionally, I'd go with him to an "open meeting." When he was sober he was caring and fun and we were a happy family. Fire Island was our greatest joy – to hear the surf pounding as you fell asleep in Pop's cottage and to swim in the surf the next morning. At night we'd put a Coleman lantern on the front of a dingy and hunt for eels in the tall grassy edges of the bay. We'd tread for clams in our bare feet and catch crabs just as they sped. Sometimes Alfred joined us and "played his nets" in the Bay to catch weakfish. We'd eat pans of fish roe fried with potatoes and onions to golden brown. In the fall, the men would bring their two

Model-T trucks to the ocean side, and with one end of the huge net attached to one truck, they'd run the net out in a giant semi-circle returning to shore where the second truck was parked. When the end was fastened to his truck, they would move both trucks slowly back toward the dunes, hauling in great sea-bass which were packed in ice and sent to the Fulton Street Fish Market in New York City. The work was hard and exhausting, but no one complained. They were all drawn to the sea like the great gulls that hovered above them as they worked. We all loved Fire Island; still do. There, the lovely landscape stretched for miles. All of life's traumas were obliterated for an hour or a day or a week. We crossed the bay in storms, in sunshine, in moonlight and on ice. The heartbeat of the Atlantic has never left me.

The Ackerly men were strong men. They fought to win. Sea and sand bound them together like nothing else. They thrived on the beer-filled bravado of their claims to the greatest catch, or finest race, in the Ackerly kitchen or in the waterfront bars.

But even the ocean failed to tame the demons of alcoholism. Perhaps it even fueled it. The scenes grew wilder. There were spells of sobriety, then long separations, hospitalizations for dt's (delirium tremens), physical and mental abuse, and promises, promises, promises. When Carol's life was threatened, I left for good. If it hadn't been for my education and knowledge that I could support Carol, I might never have made that final break ...or we might both be dead.

Why do women stay so long?

They've been made to feel inadequate and to blame for it all, that's why. Who was to blame? I don't know if any one person was or ever is. I do know that alcoholism is a disease that can only be cured by abstinence – *total* abstinence – and even then it isn't really cured; it's in remission, waiting for the first drink to start the reaction again. Sooner or later it sadly will.

Abstinence! Dad was an alcoholic. He abstained for years and lived a quiet life but one day he decided it wouldn't hurt just to have "one drink." He was so thirsty. As with every alcoholic, it never ends with "just one drink" and he was soon at it again. It wasn't just his life that he ruined, it was ours, too. Mom, Muriel and I all suffered for his giving in to his disease. But, like Nelson, it was always his needs that must be met. I believe he loved us all but he didn't know how to share that with us.

Nelson and I sold our home on Hawkins Hill and I took Carol and went back to teaching in West Babylon. Before our divorce was finalized, Nelson had remarried. He made one partial support payment for Carol and then never sent another cent. Carol can probably count the times that he made any effort to see her. One of these was when his first grandchild, Michele, was born. His family members have told me that he did love and miss Carol. Like I said, most alcoholics have trouble letting loved ones know that they care. Once they figure that out, their recovery usually improves. Usually.

Carol and I moved into a small apartment in West Bablyon and I taught in the Main Street School. She entered first grade there. Within the year I met Vic Rothermel: coach, physical education teacher, gymnast. On vacations, Vic worked for Mr. Entenmann in his small Bay Shore bakery. Yes, the same one that now sells coast to coast. Vic was divorcing his wife, although they still lived in the same house. She had long since stopped sleeping in the same bed with him. Friends told me that she was constantly depressed and difficult to be around. We began to date steadily and when his divorce was final we were married and a baby boy (Leonard) was on the way! We moved to Miami and lived in a small cottage behind Merle's home that she and Bart owned. Vic underwent surgery before we left Long Island to remove most of his stomach and he could no longer coach. There were few jobs of any kind in Florida in the early 50's. Vic did all sorts of work from cleaning toilets in restaurants to pool work. We finally both got teaching jobs in North Florida. He was grateful to teach science and health as well as physical education. We moved to Trenton, Florida in 1954 and as his strength returned, he began coaching the midget football team there. Within a few years he was one of the top referees in the state for the basketball tournaments.

Before we lived in Trenton, our life had been hell. We were cramped into a tiny cottage, no air conditioning, ants, snakes and scorpions in and out, Carol had to eat food totally foreign to her at school (grits, greens, pork fat soaked potatoes) and hated it. I packed her lunches but it didn't erase the fact that she had been moved about once too often. She had been cared for by Mom, by three different nursery schools, by Alice Ackerly, Barbara Ackerly, Mom Ackerly, Josie Redding; had been moved into nine different homes or apartments that I can remember; all by the time she was seven. She definitely developed an *attitude*. I was too weak from lack of proper food and severe anemia to deal with it. Vic was impatient with her. He felt the guilt of leaving his own daughter Susie. Leonard was not progressing physically as he should. He was malnourished, wouldn't eat, ran high fevers. I had to go to work to put food on the table. Once we both had jobs, things began to improve. For one thing, we could afford proper medical care.

Mom was still living at Wildfields. Aunt Margaret, Uncle Nard, David and Barnell in the "Old House." Grandpa held his own at Wildfields while Mom went to work. I have so few strong memories of Burnell because when I left Long Island at seventeen to go to college, he was just seven years old. He played with his friends and fought constantly with David. But I do remember his smile. He was a really skinny kid with blond hair and his great grin.

One time when Burnell was high school age, I was dating Vic and we had parked on the roadside near the little red barn to talk and "neck" before going home. Burnell and a friend suddenly appeared at the car window and, with great bravado, Burnell loudly yelled in, "Get out of here. This is private property!" Then he saw my face appear and embarrassed and apologizing, backed away. We gave up our "love making" amidst waves of laughter.

Florida was difficult! No money – no work for Vic who couldn't yet coach. I cashed in my life insurance and we lived on mashed potatoes, canned tomatoes and coffee and milk for days. I really was hungry, often giving my portion to the two children to fill them up. Trenton was a blessing. We could pay bills again. It was a small country town west of Gainesville, Florida: a farming community with watermelons, cucumbers and strawberries exported. There were a few cattle farms and a few peanut and tobacco farms. Most raised their own corn, soybeans, black-eyed peas, okra and collard greens. There were more churches than stores, a black section with its own school, a white school laid out campus-style, and the county court house right in the center of town. Trenton was the crossroads of north-south, Highway 129 and east-west, Highway 26 which ran through Gainesville and joined Route 75 northwest to the panhandle. It was a tiny town filled with good hard-working people. It was true that most were racist. They had grown up with those beliefs and little outside influence. This issue finally made life there unbearable for me though and we returned north in 1959.

Vic taught science in Trenton High School and coached the midget football team. I taught first grade. The Suwannee River was just a few miles away and we swam in the cold, cold springs. We even grew black-eyed peas and ate them with chili sauce as the natives did. We drove to the beach at Cedar Key on the Gulf of Mexico and ate catfish, corn bread and hushpuppies there. Once we were sharecroppers with a family whose son was in Vic's class. We put in the money for seeds and fertilizer and it doubled when the crop of peanuts came in. In Trenton, peanuts were boiled not roasted. They, along with pecans, were a great fall crop. In summer our backyard was piled high with watermelons that friends gave us: huge, luscious, crisp Charleston grays and cannonballs. We made the long ten hour drove to Miami to visit Muriel and Merle, and they also came to us. Mom left Wildfields after Grandpa died and was living in Trenton with us, caring for Leonard who was too young for school and had physical problems caused by cerebral palsy. When Leonard was about four, we put him in Mrs. Buchanan's Nursery School. She later became nanny to the Florida governor's children. Vic's brother Leonard and sister Ethel with her husband, Harold, and daughter, Harriet, came to visit. Cousin Edith spent weeks with us, leaving the cold north behind. My friend May Lynch from my college days visited as did Julie and Bob Heath and Alice Ackerly. Ruth Ackerly often came in her trailer home with husband, Frank Abramo. Mom Ackerly stayed with us once. These were ties that were so important to us to keep. Except for Christmas, none of us heard from Wildfields.

Almost everyone in Trenton turned out for the football games which were held at night. During one half-time, Vic and the head coach of the high school team, Coach Patricka, provided the entertainment with an enactment of "Zorro" on horseback. Vic borrowed the horse he rode and the only available saddle was a much-too-small English saddle. After one afternoon rehearsal, Vic was very blistered and so he cushioned his rear that night with some of my Kotex, fearing that when he dismounted they'd fall out and provide even more entertainment! Except for his sore buttocks, it went smoothly. I still have the tiny cheerleader's jacket that Leonard wore to those night games when he could barely walk.

The kids adored Vic. He was gregarious and fun-loving. In one of the midget football games, his fastest runner, Gene Corbin, heading down the field for a touchdown saw Vic along the stretch and waving his free arm called out, "Hi Coach!" A great tribute, but it's lucky for him that he made that touchdown. He'd have faced a wrath unseen before had he not.

Vic and Carol often rode horseback together. Her love of horses grew there as did her love of boys! Many girls, developing early in this hot climate, were having babies at fourteen or fifteen. The Beatles long hair began to have its influence. Adults were literally horrified. Until then weekly haircuts were a must. Boys who let their hair grow were considered inappropriate partners by adults and daughters were warned to stay away from them. Elvis and The Everly Brothers were heard everywhere. The rural twang of country music was overtaken by new sounds.

Segregation issues were more and more prominent in these rural towns that had never known anything but racial division. The old worn-out books in the white school were tied up and sent to the black school across town. It was common and acceptable to hire black women to care for the most precious of possessions – the children. But it wasn't okay for black and white children to play together. One teacher buried an arsenal of guns and ammunition just outside the agricultural building on campus for, "the days when someone sits a black next to my kid in school." The marches to Selma were not that far away. I wanted to join them. Even the Florida Education Association took a stand for segregation and told us their *recommended* way to vote. I was working on my Master's Degree at Gainesville University and Leonard's disabilities were becoming more and more apparent making it difficult to leave home and travel the thirty miles to the university at night. Vic's growing aggravation with a teenage Carol made it even harder!

Then changes came to Wildfields. Grandpa, Ethelbert Hawkins Selleck, died in 1955 at age the age of 89. Mom came to Florida to live with us. Aunt Margaret and Uncle Nard and the boys moved into Wildfields. (Dave recently told me that he had already moved in before Mom left because kids taunted him about living in that old house: Merritt Hawkins Homestead. Both of the houses and acres of adjoining property were left to Aunt Margaret and Uncle Nard. Mom received bordering acreage around Wildfields.

Vic and Muriel's husband, Russell Tierney, made a memorable trip north to retrieve Mom's car and what possessions she could claim as her own. Towing a U-haul with Vic driving his car, and Russell driving Mom's, they left Long Island with as many of her dearest possessions as would fit, piled high in the U-haul. When they got to the Lincoln Tunnel, they started into it going the wrong way, and were abruptly stopped by police who were screaming at them.

"Where in hell do you think you're going?" A burly cop yelled in Vic's window. Vic explained that he and Russ were returning to Florida with their mother-in-law's car and furniture.

"And who the hell are all these people behind you?" Turning, Vic saw a stream of cars that had followed them there. The tunnel was tied up for some time while they turned them all around. Muriel and I were never told if they were issued tickets.

With Mom living with us we could leave Leonard at home and not send him out to a babysitter. He was very thin and frail after running fevers of 104 to 105. Because of the cerebral palsy, he was prone to respiratory ailments, ear and stomach infections. One Gainesville physician labeled him retarded. I knew he wasn't but he did have neurological disabilities. He had small seizures which eventually turned from petit mal to grand mal when he reached puberty. He was diagnosed at Sunland Training Center in Gainesville and the brain damage was pin-pointed to the right parental area of his brain. Seizures showed up every few seconds at times on his EEG.

A year after Grandpa died, Uncle Nard died of cancer, leaving Aunt Margaret and the two boys alone at Wildfields. Both David and Burnell had graduated from Colgate University. Burnell took a job at Brookhaven Laboratory on Long Island and married his childhood sweetheart from just down Pond Path, Alice Holgersons. They raised a family of three boys. Later they moved to Rochester where Burnell got his doctoral degree, and then to Michigan where he taught in Michigan State University at Lansing.

David married Barbara Hang and moved into a cape cod-style home in Westchester County, town of Pelham, New York, where he taught science in New Rochelle at the junior high level until he retired in 1995.

As the boys moved away, Aunt Margaret was left alone at Wildfields. Bravely, she returned to college at C.W. Post in Westbury and got her Master's Degree in Reading. Previously, she had taught business subjects in Port Jefferson High School, and then worked as a secretary to Dr. Gabelein at the Stony Brook school. Eventually she would commute the distance to West Babylon schools as I had done years before. She taught there until she retired. How lovely it must have been at Wildfields, getting up at 5AM on cold winter mornings, arriving home at dark to prepare and eat a meal alone. She was then a women in her sixties and found no leftover energy to participate in local activities except for church. That's also where her strength came from, her faith!

By 1959, Muriel and Merle had established families in Miami. Muriel and Russ had three children: Margaret, Frank Russell III, and Kevin. Russ worked in the post office. Merle had married Bartlett Tuthill Brown and also had three children: Michael, Linda and Kathy. Bart was a carpenter who did excellent work and Merle a nurse in the local hospitals. She was, in fact, working at Jackson Memorial Hospital in Miami when Leonard was born there.

Florida left much to be desired, but not the school system however. They were advanced beyond the New York System at the time that we lived there in many ways (one of which was not salaries!) It was the social issues, lack of work for Vic, and the endless humidity and heat that made me long for the Northeast. Vic and I sent applications all over New York's eastern area (we were still licensed to teach in New York) and in April of 1959 came on our spring break for interviews. We chose Middletown of all the places who offered us both teaching jobs; the very city where Grandpa had grown up and in which his parents had owned a store some one-hundred years ago!

In 1959 Middletown, New York was a small city of about 25,000 with one high school, a new junior high, and five or six elementary schools. We bought a home on East Main Street, just at the city's edge. Carol was in junior High, where Vic would be teaching science. Leonard was starting first grade in the school on Albert Street where I taught third grade. We had a lovely two-story home with a vast yard and great neighbors. Carol walked to school; Len went with me. Mom had lunch ready for Len and me each day as there was no cafeterias in Albert Street School. Len immediately became friends with Jackie Jacobs whose parents had escaped death in the concentration camps of W.W.II. The two of them are still friends today. Jackie is married with two children, living in Ohio. His mom, Jennie, still lives in Middletown. His dad, Ben, died years ago. Jenny *never* talks of the horrors of the past but the tattooed numbers on her arm are tell-tale.

On our way to Middletown from Florida we tried to locate Mom's roots in Newark, New Jersey. She was so shocked and saddened by the deterioration of the whole area that she begged us to go on without ever locating her old street. We were close enough for her to see what it would be like.

Mom's health was also deteriorating. She spent her days feeding the cats, sewing, and awaiting our return from the schools. The doctor had given her orders not to do any strenuous work and so all of that was left for me. As Carol got older she helped. Vic kept the lawns trimmed and in the summer he took a job at Lloyds department store. Carol babysat locally and eventually took a job in a downtown department store. Her attitude was typical of the 60's era: leave me alone to find myself and give me all freedoms. She wasn't a hippie; in fact, she dressed quite conservatively. She just never felt loved; never felt whole.

As Mom was hospitalized more and more for heart problems, we realized that she couldn't be left alone. Occasionally we got her to her beloved Long Island for short visits. She'd wish, "If only we could live there again." She began to sell off the acreage she'd inherited and offered us the lot nearest the barn. We could barely keep up with our Middletown expenses and it wasn't zoned for summer cottages, so we turned her down. About seven years later we did move back to Long Island and had to buy our present property! How I've wished that she had lived to be here with us, but it was only my inheritance from her that made it possible to be here now. Maybe she sees it clearly from wherever she is!

Mom died in 1965 when that tired heart finally gave out. She was seventy years old. The funeral was held at O.B. Davis funeral parlor then on East Main Street in Port Jefferson, NY. (The O.B. in O.B. Davis stands for Orlando Burnell Davis, by the way). A winter storm piled snow high on this January the 12th, and we stood in the cemetery of the Presbyterian churchyard in Setauket, shivering with cold. Vic was very quiet. His relationship with his mother-in-law had been one of love. Mom often said that Vic reminded her of my dad. He did to me, too. For forty-two years Mom had instilled in me the faith that has forever sustained me. She was the greatest role model for courage that I've ever known. Timid, anxious, caring, insecure – all described her, but under it all was raw courage with a determined belief. She scrubbed floors, sorted hospital linens, put rivets in airplanes, was maid and housekeeper to the rich, secretary, bookkeeper, nurses aide, loving daughter, loving mother, loving grandmother, loving friend and above all else: a Christian. She never had her own home but it didn't matter; she loved Wildfields so much. I wonder if she didn't *spiritually* lead me back home.

By 1964 Merle had been diagnosed terminally ill with cancer. She and Bart and their three beautiful children were living in Miami, Florida. Bart had property in Eastport, Long Island and he moved a two-story home from the main street to his lot on Tuthill Road, across from the side of the Eastport school. Merle had inherited land from her father and had sold it to the board of education of the Three Village School District. The Nassakeag Elementary School was built there in the early sixties. Bart, carpenter by trade, stopped working to care for Merle and their two girls. Merle's inheritance was, therefore, dwindling rapidly. She wanted Bart to work, saying she could get through each day and at that point, she could. Merle and Bart returned to Long Island before the Eastport home was ready to live in. Merle stayed with her friend, Mary Reboli, so that she could get chemotherapy at Brookhaven Lab. Bart remained in Eastport to work on the house and the girls, Linda and Kathy, stayed in Middletown with me. I had registered to work on my Master's Degree at New Paltz State Teachers College (now SUNY at New Paltz) that summer but quickly withdrew to care for the girls. Vic put a small pool in the backyard which Kathy and Leonard enjoyed, but poor Linda had gotten plantars warts and had to keep her feet dry. We made regular visits to the doctor to have them burned away. Merle was so ill. She visited once or twice but barely had the strength to put the girls to bed. Mickey returned from Florida in time to celebrate his and Kathy's birthday on August 20th and shortly after that they all returned to Florida. Merle, knowing how ill she was, felt that she might never return to live in the Eastport house and begged me, as we sat talking throughout the night, to watch over the girls. That was something that Bart made it impossible to do. I shall always regret that.

The next January, Mom died and Merle was too ill to return for her funeral. Mom was "Aunt Effie" to all of Bernard's children. She did her best to care for them when their mothers were unable to do so.

In early summer, Merle and her family did return to Long Island. Bart had the house in Eastport beautifully finished with a bedroom and bath downstairs for Merle.

"I can see my piano from the doorway," she told me. "Now if I just had the strength to walk over and play it!"

That summer the girls and Mickey stayed in Eastport and we traveled to them. I drove down every Saturday to see them, often alone. Merle's cancer spread throughout her body, great lumps appearing in her neck, chest and back. She would beg me to stay after the evening shot of morphine, saying she would get ill. Once she fell asleep I'd leave. It was a long, lonely ride back to Middletown on those Saturday nights.

Just before Thanksgiving, Merle died on November 20th, 1965. Eleven years later, Bart died – on the very same day – of a blood clot following cancer surgery. It was almost two years later before we bonded with Merle's girls again and were now living in Setauket again. Linda, married to George Baldo, has a son Jesse and they live in a lovely two-story home on land between Upper and Lower Sheep Pasture Roads once owned by Grandpa. We are within walking distance of one another.

Linda went into nursing following in her mother's footsteps and she set up the 5th floor Oncology Unit at St. Charles Hospital in Port Jefferson. (A place I visited as a patient all too frequently from 1991 to 1994). She's bright and compassionate, as was her mother. George has his doctorate from nearby Stony Brook University and does research in the medical center there as a Biophysicist. Jesse, their son, attends the Nassakeag Elementary School on land sold to the school district by his grandmother and owned by his ancestors for eight generations before that.

Michael Brown (Mickey) lives in Florida. He married, had a daughter Arlyn and was divorced. He received his law degree at the University of Florida at Gainesville and practices in St. Petersburg. He will soon remarry.

Kathy married Rob Polack and lives either in her Fort Lee, New Jersey, apartment or her Remsenberg Long Island home, near Eastport. She was a model for a time. Rob travels a great deal, going to Europe or the Far East for his jewelry business.

Linda and George have joined our Methodist church where George set up the acoustic system and Linda adds her lovely voice to the choir. George's mom is a generous, caring person. How often Della Baldo has helped me! She's smart, pretty and fun to be with. When Della's husband, Sully, was terminally ill with cancer, Linda was one of his nurses at St. Charles Hospital and it was there that she met George (déjà vu: Merle met Bart when he was a patient at Mather Hospital down the block).

Sometimes I feel that Merle is very close to us. She'd be so happy to know that her girls were a part of our lives, and Mickey's when he's north! Muriel's children are far from Wildfields. Her daughter, Margaret, was born with a disability – part of one leg was missing. Her leg was amputated and she's never used a prosthesis successfully and gets around on crutches. She works for Sound Security at Baltimore and visits often. Kevin, Jennie and their son, Cameron, live in or near Denver. He works for Blue Cross. (Years go by before he can get East.) Jay (Frank Russell Tierney III) recently remarried. He has two grown sons by his first marriage, Michael and Jonathan. He visited with his new wife, Barbara, whom we all adored. Margaret – Margie to most of us – is an artist in her own right; she sketches beautifully. We've all become close friends of Joseph Reboli (a talented local artist) and Margie commissioned Joe to do oil paintings of the "Old House" and Wildfields. While he was working on these, he gave me a watercolor he did of the backdoor at Wildfields. This is one of a very few watercolors that he has done. I've taken oil painting lessons from Joe. Now I'm doing an oil painting of Wildfields which I hope to put on the cover of this rambling memoir. Mary was Joe's aunt.

Muriel and I became closer and closer as we became adults. We spent almost every one of my vacations together at one place or another. One summer Leonard and I joined Muriel at Camp Hill and with Kevin, she drove us to Cowan's Gap on Tuscarora Mountain in Pennsylvania – near Chambersburg. Margie drove up from Baltimore where she worked. Muriel rented a cabin from the state and we split costs. It was a beautiful place. Great trees surrounded us. The path leading to a man-made lake was strewn with boulders. We had a large central room with a huge fireplace and kitchen and bedroom for Muriel and Margie, two other bedrooms with upper and lower bunks with walls going only three-quarters of the way up. I could lean out of my upper berth and talk to Muriel who was on the couch in the living room below. We shared an outdoor privy out in the woods, somewhere down the path, and it was indeed shared by people who slipped by in the night leaving the odor of marijuana heavy in the summer air.

One night we drove back to the campground headquarters at lakeside. We sat in Muriel's station wagon yodeling, laughing and singing. Margie still yodels when she calls me on the phone from Baltimore. It's her "opening theme." Kevin and Leonard searched the woods and waters for the miracles of nature. The kind of good life that never should have ended.

The next year I rented the cabin from New York State at Copake Falls. Another joyous adventure. Carol and Michele visited us from Middletown.

Soon after that I spoke with Muriel via phone. She said she was going to the doctor that day because she had discovered a lump under her arm, and he would do an aspiration.

"Please, God," I thought, "not cancer again!" It was about ten years since Merle had died of it. The next day I called Muriel to see what diagnosis the doctor had given. "It's probably cancer," she said. "I'll know in two days, but the doctor believes it is."

"How is Russell taking it?" I asked.

"He didn't ask the results," she answered. "He wanted to go shopping and never asked, and I dammed well won't tell him until he does!"

In the year that followed, I spent as much time as possible of my vacations at Camp Hill. Muriel came to Long Island when Margie drove her; once she flew up from Harrisburg. She felt fairly good that summer of 1974. We went to craft fairs, took her to the ocean, ate at waterfront restaurants, watched the Watergate scandal develop, walked across the fields and down to the pond and talked our way back through time.

In October Russ called and asked me to fly down to Camp Hill for a weekend. Muriel was sick and weak from chemotherapy but strong enough to take me on a drive to see the new Susquehanna River Bridge! If it wasn't the sewer system being put in on her street, it was the Three Mile Island nuclear plant or a new bridge that held her interest! She should have been an engineer.

Russ set up a room in the basement of their home and he slept there so I could be with Muriel. He was, he thought, Lord of the Manor and no one would *ever* infringe on his rights or his home. If anyone came on his property he said he'd shoot them and drag the body inside and say that they had invaded his home! He nailed all of the first floor windows shut, which would be outrageous when Mom lived there and needed fresh air to be able to breath freely. Well, one night, Muriel and I lay talking when we heard disturbing noises outside on the front sidewalk. A young man and a girl were having a heated argument. It was very late and the argument escalated into her screams. Muriel called the police. Bonnie, the dog, barked wildly. When the police arrived and came in, the dog was beside herself. We spoke with the police, telling them the girl had run into the backyard, with the man running after her, and they had disappeared into someone else's yard. The police finally left not having found her, and we fell asleep, but not until we laughed hysterically at the fact that Russ hadn't even known that the police were there. He was snoring away in the basement the whole time.

We didn't say a word about it the next day but the neighbors saw Russ outside and called over to him. "Wasn't that some excitement last night at your house!"

So much for protecting ones property from intruders! Russ barely spoke to us all day because if he so much as looked at us, we broke into gales of laughter.

In November, Vic, Leonard and I drove to Camp Hill and to Dillsburg to be with Susy, Vince and Krista. Muriel was in the hospital because her white blood count had dropped so low from chemotherapy. She had been in isolation but was back in a regular room. I called the doctors from Hershey Medical Center who were her Oncologists and they verified my fears – that time was running out. She was so pale and thin. I wanted to just hold on to her and never let go.

At Christmas, we went to Camp Hill for the entire vacation. Muriel was back home, propped up in a hospital bed in the downstairs sunporch, her head in a turban.

"My head freezes," she said smiling. "How did Grandpa ever stand it!" (I came to know just what she meant and felt the same way in July.)

Some of us went to Trinity Lutheran Church, where she was a member, for the Christmas Eve service. Shortly after we returned, a group of carolers arrived. What joy that brought her.

Margie was working in Baltimore, Jay in Pittsburg. He and his wife, Mercedes, and son, Michael, arrived for Christmas. Russ flittered around sometimes incoherent, popping pills, drinking coffee, giving orders to anyone or no one in particular. Kevin was a senior in high school and worked in a grocery store nearby. Muriel worried constantly about his future, his friends, his pot smoking, his not filling out forms for college. Before the week was over, she was taken by ambulance to the hospital in Harrisburg. Russ determined when and who could visit her. He gave me priority over his kids; was terribly abrupt and mean to Mercedes. I shared a room with her and Mickie, and heard her upset in the night.

In January, I drove to Camp Hill again. This time I was alone. I went to Muriel's room in the hospital. She was sleeping but soon awoke.

"Would you wash my teeth?" she asked. "They never remember."

I did and returned them to her. "Leave them out," she said. "I can't eat anyhow."

The doctor came in and I removed myself to the hall bench where I could still see her – her tiny frame, her bald head (she'd long since discarded her wig), her pale gray face. A man walked his young wife down the hall and when she saw me she said, "She's so sweet. Is she your mother?"

"She's only fifty-three," I said. "She's my sister."

I fought the tears, and I saw the expression in her face of things to come.

When I returned to Muriel's bedside she said, "You know – this dying isn't so bad."

Not for you perhaps, dear sister. Just for us.

I knew I'd seen her for the last time. On January 22nd, 1975 she died, just three days after I left her side. Her ashes were scattered at the Assateague Island Wildlife Refuge, a place she dearly loved, right next to where the wild ponies of Chincoteague still roam.

In 1964, I was dealing with Vic's illness as well as Mom's and Merle's. Vic was finding teaching in Middletown New York more and more "hazardous to his health." He began to have less control with drinking and we went through some wild experiences. Russ had loaned him a gun for which no one had a permit. One of his wildest moments involved this gun and sent Leonard and I to our friends, Julie and Bob Heath, and Carol to her boyfriends, Don Weiser (whom she later married). Bob Heath returned to our house to try and calm Vic down before he killed himself or someone else. Vic had already driven off. But Bob found the gun and brought it to me. Julie and I, in our usual insane fashion, decided to dispose of it. It was a very dark night and we chose the Wallkill River to be its final resting place. We parked the car next to what appeared to be a totally isolated area and got out, heading toward the river bank through thick weeds and underbrush ready to heave the gun into the murky waters. Within moments, a chorus of baying hounds and deep barks reached our ears. Lights went on in a nearby house that was hidden in the darkness from our view. The barking got closer. Much closer! We turned and ran, snagging our clothes, as fast as we could, jumped in the car and headed back to Julie's – with the gun.

Russ Tierney drove up from Camp Hill that same night, found Vic in a Port Jervis bar and brought him home. The gun went back to Pennsylvania.

The stress and pressure of school were obviously getting to Vic. He was used to being in his own confined classroom where he methodically did an excellent job of teaching science. But "team teaching" was introduced and he couldn't function with new young teachers with new ideas and new methods. He drank more and more. Some of the episodes were even funny, like his afternoon on the ride-on lawn mower, riding wildly around our two acres — flowers and shrubbery strewn along the way!

One day in 1967, we had made a trip to Long Island and stopped at the model homes being built on what had been Mom's land behind Wildfields. We loved the ranch model, and upon our return to Middletown discussed the possibility of leaving there and building on that property. Carol had married Don Weiser at age nineteen and had a baby girl. Leonard was in junior high school. He was diagnosed with cerebral palsy and epilepsy. (A diagnosis of depression was yet to come). Vic was dissatisfied and I just loved Long Island. We decided to try it and sent out job applications in the area of Setauket and nearby villages. Our home at 324 East Main Street went up for sale. Long Island was changing rapidly; developments were springing up everywhere including Mom's property around Wildfields which she had sold. There were only one or two lots left – one directly behind Wildfields behind what was Grandpa's garden. God must have been holding it for us. We bought it and by August 1967 we moved into 8 Storybook Lane, Setauket, New York. The three houses stood in a row from west to east: the Merritt Hawkins homestead ("the Old House"), Wildfields, and 8 Storybook Lane. I had come home.

The three houses covered a span of 165 years. Aunt Margaret Selleck had renovated the first floor of the "Old House" and rented it. She lived alone at Wildfields and seemed so happy to have our presence so close. She still drove to West Babylon where she taught business subjects in the high school under Vic's friend, Helmer Petersen. She retired at age sixty-five. Vic obtained a teaching position in Centereach and I was to teach second grade in Port Jefferson Station at the Terryville school.

When Grandpa's property was divided, following his death, there was much animosity between Aunt Margaret and Mom, but I was determined to heal any lingering, unnecessary wounds. They weren't my wounds. We moved into our new home in August, just in time to unpack, put up drapes, shades, curtains, arrange and rearrange furniture. Then the schools opened and we were immersed in our routines again.

Muriel and Margie came to visit. Margie sewed cottage curtains for me from a bright flowered material I had bought in Patchogue. One clear night, Muriel and I were leaning on the dining room window sills looking out and up at a star-filled sky, quiet and crystal clear; filled with peace. Now a great Norway maple tree fills that space and the stars are hidden in the neon glow of malls and the University at Stony Brook. The owl we heard is quiet and can no longer find a home here. The paths dad walked to the rail road station are covered with homes and dorms and the hospital grounds. Long Island was still somewhat rural when we came back in 1967. Grandpa had allowed Al Hobbs to plow the fields and plant crops and he still does. It kept the weeds down for Aunt Margaret and David, but it took away the daisies and golden rod that I loved to see. We spent hours landscaping the yard; we planted seedlings from the mother spruce that lined the northern side of Wildfields. Vic bought ornamental trees: Quansan cherry, Japanese crab apple, golden maple, black pine silver maple and corkscrew willow. We transplanted birch and dogwood from the fields at Wildfields and lilac and myrtle and trumpet vine from the "Old House" yard. Aunt Margaret would go with me and tell me what clumps I could have – clumps of my life – the bond between childhood and today. The yard became so overcrowded that a teacher friend, Leslie Tuthill, told me she always wanted to bring her class here when they studied the rain forest!

Three months after I started teaching at the Terryville Elementary School, I had to have surgery and I was out of school for many weeks. The day after I returned to school, Vic had a complete breakdown and left his job. He just walked out. Leonard found junior high an emotional horror. He was taunted by bullies for weeks until he finally hit the ringleader with his lunch bag which held a can of juice or soda. Vic tried to commit suicide by using the vacuum hose in the car, but I stopped him and he committed himself to Suffolk Psychiatric Ward for about two months. I took in a Chinese couple that Aunt Margaret sent over to help with the bills. The husband was a university student; the wife was pregnant and rarely left her room, which was my room previously. Vic returned home a broken piece of a man. He never taught school again. After thirty-four years of teaching, he went out on a disability pension of $156 a month, diagnosed a manic-depressive. I tried to give him things to do during the day, but things just got worse. One doctor told me, "Just don't give into his moods."

"You live with him," I thought. He had no medication except aspirin which he took constantly.

One day we took Leonard to the family doctor for a sore throat and cold. A few days later, since he was worse, he said to come pick up a prescription for a different antibiotic. His office was on Hallock Road – a five- or ten-minute ride away. We had been there many times in the past on our way to the Smithhaven Mall. Vic went for the medicine. Over two hours passed before he returned. "I couldn't find the doctor's office!" he screamed. He had ended up at MacArthur Airport and then had driven into Nassau County where police helped him find his way back. He was seriously ill. He was despondent. He was sure he'd totally let us down. He took whatever work he could find. He worked at Mather Hospital for a short time, and then as a security guard at several places until his problems with cardiovascular disease prompted his complete retirement. He could barely walk and when he became bedridden, I hired aides to come in during the day; I cared for him at night. Teach was a nightmare. Gangrene set in his right foot. Hid kidneys began to shut down. He was incontinent. On January 26, 1978, his frail body went by ambulance to St. Charles Hospital in Port Jefferson where he died the next morning.

Everyone goes through these trials. What sustains us? Vic, when he could still stand on his hurting legs, stood at his dresser every evening reading from the big white family Bible. I sat quietly at the kitchen table every morning and prayed. God gave us both the strength we asked for. And I thanked him for my health and my job. I loved teaching. Our faculty room was like a family gathering. We shared all hopes, dreams, sorrows, joys and laughter. We still do. We carried on worse than the children in the halls outside. We loved parties. We loved each other.

When I came home, I still had Leonard and Wildfields was just beyond the gate. I wandered the beaches. No longer could I see the porpoise leaping as we had when were children at West Meadows, but the same ancient waters lapped at my feet and the sunsets were as glorious as ever.

In 1975 Leonard graduated from SUNY at Stony Brook. Our dreams were fulfilled when we saw him get his diploma. After receiving his bachelor's in economics, he went to Suffolk Community College and earned an associate's degree in accounting. His father's illness exacerbated his emotional fragility and genetic tendency; it was evident that he, too, had clinical depression.

Grandpa's land became full-blown suburbia: with homes, yards, people and cars. But I could always look out of the western windows and see nothing but fields and hedges and Wildfields, and the chaos ceased to exist.

Raccoons, which Leonard named banditos, came to the bird feeders. One summer a mama raccoon brought her three babies to us. Our grandchildren were visiting and Marc, Lisa and Michele fed them bread with peanut butter and honey. Father Bandito got into the garage and nestled in the crowded space above the kitchen sink each day when the garage door was up. A baby bandito crawled into the chimney and slept on the flue. We routed him with smoke and he appeared at the top of the chimney, rubbing his eyes. Jim Clancy, art teacher and friend, covered the chimney with wire and later I had caps put on it. Someone once put cowbells on all of the babies. They got into the attic crawl space and we heard them racing about overhead as we sat in the den. As the University Medical Center was being built they – or their cousins – got into the rafters, tails hanging down into the unfinished office ceilings. They were great fun but too rambunctious and destructive. As fields and woodlands were destroyed to build homes, the raccoons had no place to go and left us. Occasionally some would show up on Dave's property or on our front porch if cat food was left out there. An opossum or two ate at the bird feeder and the yard was filled with squirrels and birds which I fed – and still feed to this day. Life centered on my home, our survival and my family still in Middletown. Every month or two, Leonard and I drove to see Carol, her husband and the three grandchildren. We alternated holidays. Aunt Margaret left to visit her family in Michigan every summer and we watched over Wildfields. David, who now lived in Pelham, came out often. Sometimes his wife Barbara and three children were with him. I'd always see Aunt Margaret's lights on when I got up each morning. She was always up first! On Labor Day she gathered Dave and family, Vic, Leonard and me on her side porch for a shared meal. When Russell Sorensen, her brother, came to visit her, we would gather here. Sometimes her sister, Martha, came and I'd go and get her from the airport. No one comes anymore. Aunt Margaret lives with Burnell in Michigan where he teachers at Michigan State. Her memory is gone as she struggles with Alzheimer's and Alice and Burnell share the grave responsibility of her constant care.

At about the same time that Aunt Margaret left Wildfields, I discovered that I had breast cancer. I now had the same battle to fight that had defeated Muriel and Merle. Great medical strides had been made since their deaths (Merle died of ovarian cancer and Muriel of breast cancer) and my care was quite different. My surgeon, Dr. Ziviello, removed the tumor and lymph nodes at St. Charles Hospital where Merle's daughter, Linda, works. The follow up was six months of chemotherapy and six and a half weeks of radiation under the wonderful care of my oncologist, Dr. Joan Dobbs. Della Baldo took me to my first appointment and the dear, dear friend that she is has helped me in so many ways ever since.

My hair came out, leaving just a few wisps; I bought a wig. I cried.

In early November of 1991 my therapy was over. Great bleeding blisters and burns covered my armpit and right side and under my breast. God again gave me the strength that I prayed for to get through it. It healed. I felt healthy again. All that winter, spring, and summer of 1992, I went about – business as usual. Aunt Margaret grew progressively worse. She would phone me from Wildfields a dozen times in the morning to ask what day it was (even though David had bought a large kitchen wall clock with the date on it!) I walked over every day to spend time with her. I'd make myself a cup of instant coffee and make her a cup of Postum and we'd try our best to carry on a conversation. She wouldn't let me use her soap to wash the cups and they became so dirty that I either brought my own cup or dish detergent to clean things up. She was growing very thin and obviously not eating properly. Meals on Wheels came at noon and ran into their own problems with her disease. They would drive over to my house to tell me that they could get no answer at the door and I'd grab my key and run across the field to Wildfields. I'd usually find her sound asleep on the living room couch. They discussed dropping her from their rounds because she was holding them up from delivering hot meals to others. Dave then hired Lorraine Mattwell (Joseph Matusky's daughter) to come an hour before Meals on Wheels was due, to be sure she was up and ready to eat. There were Chinese graduate students living upstairs and she would lock them out. Soon she was coming to me because she couldn't get back inside after going to the mailbox (which was five or six times every afternoon). Evening meals were left uneaten as she confused the time of day once it got dark. She was very rigid with her tenants. No nonsense and she enforced those rules with vigor. In all her confusion, she was still in charge of her castle!

As the disease progressed she took in tenants that she never would have dealt with before. All were students in her plan. But things changed. One man rented Mom's old room, kept all his possessions in his car and wandered the lawns and fields at night, shouting profanities to whatever shadows lurked in his brain. The "Old House" was also rented, but these people never seemed to cause difficulties to any degree. But as she became more disoriented, she caused them problems: taking the mail, going through their garbage, walking in the middle of the road. I worried about her all the time. It was a nightmare. People in the neighborhood began calling me about her behavior.

Eventually, Burnell took Aunt Margaret from Wildfields to live with him in Michigan. Now the house was inhabited by strangers only.

In the fall of 1992, malignant tumors were found in my bladder. Dr. Richard Rose removed them twice, but the second time the fast-moving cancer had spread to the bladder lining. I started a three-month series of hospital chemotherapy treatments supervised by Dr. Dobbs which totally wiped me out. All of my hair fell out in one day, like a bird's nest lying in my hand. Back to the wig and turban days and the dehumanizing feeling that comes to a bald woman. And yes, Grandpa, my head was cold! Even in July.

The bladder had to be removed. I was operated on June, 1993, and spent twenty-one days in the hospital, nineteen without food or water except for intravenous injections. Part of my small intestine was used to become my new bladder which led to a stomach pouch. With home nursing, several transfusions, the love and support of family and friends and trust in God, I was soon up and about. Lisa and Michele drove from Albany on their days off to be with me. They fed me, cheered me on, planted my flowers, and helped Leonard. What a beautiful pair of young adults. I'll never forget their unselfish, caring ways.

Back when Merritt and Ethelbert built their homes here, families were large and clustered in the neighborhoods. There was always a young generation to help the older one. Not so anymore. Families scatter all over the United States – wherever their jobs take them. Lisa and Michele, for instance, had to travel about 200 miles to see me. Carol was about two thousand miles away. She never came.

At Wildfields, the scene was changing, too. With Aunt Margaret away, the tenants quickly took over the house – or some of them did. All sorts of disturbing things happened. A black girl who rented the northeast bedroom decided that her boyfriend, Ian, should live there, too. Ian decided that his mentally disturbed brother, Ron, should also live there, and Ron decided to bring his girlfriend. The last two often slept in Aunt Margaret's bed. Ron had been hospitalized at the University Hospital psychiatric section. The girlfriend, Shari, decided her Muslim beliefs would "cure" him more rapidly and took him out without permission. When I went on my daily trek to pick up Aunt Margaret's mail, the police were there. Ian refused to let them in. Cold days and nights I had seen Ian (and/or Ron) out on the roof outside the bathroom upstairs, dancing about, poising to jump, eating from a bowl, smoking – sometimes dressed; sometimes naked. We were sure that pot was being smoked as the cigarette were passed back and forth and in and out to someone inside.

"Get those guys out of there," the police warned. "They're bad news."

Finally returning from Michigan with his wife, mother and mother-in-law, Burnell got them out. What a relief! Once again the clothesline filled with billowing sheets and trousers, shirts and shorts slapping in the breeze as Alice and Hattie put out the wash. Loved ones roamed the yards and sat on the sunny porch, and talked and drank coffee or iced tea. For just a moment, time turned back to the Wildfields that I recognized. Burnell and Alice organized a reunion – Barbara, David, Laurie, Tim, Gloria, Charlie, Motsie, Hattie, Margie, Michele, Lisa, Adrian, Leonard, Linda, George, Jesse, Della, Gunther, Robbie, Kathy, Aunt Margaret and me. It was wonderful. O.J. Simpson was taking his infamous Bronco ride on the Los Angeles freeway that day. We watched it while awaiting the arrival of loved ones.

A few months after those unwanted tenants had moved out, Ron's girlfriend was killed when he recklessly ran a red light on Route 347. David and his university friends said that she was a beautiful person.

The reunion brought us together for the first time in years. The food was fabulous. I'm sure Alice and Burnell were exhausted. The house showed hours of hard work. Even Aunt Margaret grew weary of it all. By 8 p.m. the confusion overcame her joy and it probably was her bedtime. Most of us were sitting outside on the porch when she came to the screen door and sweetly said, "Does anyone want or need anything? Because I'm locking the doors." And she proceeded to do just that.

Today I went to the Port Jefferson Station Retired Teachers Association meeting in Bellport. I had arranged for a guest speaker, a Mr. Mervin Tillinghast, to give a talk and slide show on the history of the automobile. Even teachers never stop learning! For one thing, I never knew that cars were built in Port Jefferson. One car was made there called the Only. None of us had ever heard of it (maybe only one was made!).

I had heard Mr. Tillinghast give another lecture at the East End Retired Teachers meeting a few months back. This one was on Camp Upton and Yapank (where he formerly was the principal). The scenes had reminded me that Mom had worked as an aide in the hospital there in World War II. She stayed with Bertha Darling in Patchogue during the week so that she could take a bus to Camp Upton. How many jobs she undertook! I tried mentally to recall them all: bookkeeper and secretary, live-in caregiver to Mrs. Tuthill (where Gallery North is now), night nurse's aide to Mrs. Norton in Stony Brook, aide at Mather Hospital, housekeeper to Mr. and Mrs. Crouse – owners of Peerless Photo where she later worked with Uncle Nard in the supply department, housekeeper and nanny to the Beatty family in Shoreham, maker of satin lingerie boxes in a factory on Chicken Hill, maker of the first local plastic items in a small factory near the Museums at Stony Brook, maker of cards in a card factory in Babylon, and assembly-line worker at Republic Aircraft in Farmingdale, Long Island, and Camp Upton, of course. There was also a housekeeping job at a doctor's home in Port Jefferson, but I can't remember his name, although I know that he lived in a house near Mather Hospital.

Mr. Tillinghast also mentioned a car that I'd long forgotten. After Dad's Studebaker he bought a Whippet – that also was the *only* one around.

Grandpa had Ford Model T's in the yard which we'd crank up and get the motors chugging. One was an old truck Model T. Several of our friends had them also and I can almost feel what the bouncy ride was like. Grandpa's pride and joy was his Packard with the angel hood ornament leaning out in front. Mr. Tillinghast, who is 88, said he learned to drive in a Model T. Many of the cars we rode in had rumble seats; the front seat was enclosed and the rumble seat pulled up from the back outside. It was miserable in cold or rainy weather to have to be the couple in the rumble seat, but great on warm moonlit nights! All had running boards that you stepped on to climb into the car. Once our senior high school class went on a picnic to Montauk Point. Our advisor was Peg (Lowry) West. She was riding along, hanging on to the car standing outside on the running board, when her student driver went too fast and she was thrown off and broke her ankle. We were all warned not to do such things, but we all did them. Peg West is Barbara Tyler's (Ben's wife) mother.

Many times in the early spring of 1997, Leonard and I walked over to the field behind Wildfields and witnessed the spectacular sight of the Hale-Bopp comet streaking across the north-western sky. It was easily seen there with the naked eye – no trees or houses to block the view and but we could also see it from our driveway and, with binoculars, it was a sight never to be forgotten.

As I stood out there in the field and turned to see the rows of lights from the University Hospital at Stony Brook, I remembered another night long, long ago. In the very early 1900's Count von Zeppelin designed the first airship. When I must have been about four years old, the Graf Zeppelin was to pass over central Long Island and I was awakened and carried outside to see it (as I'm sure Muriel and Merle were, too). It was like a huge flying watermelon with lights running along the side, droning heavily throughout its journey overhead. I can remember where we stood – next to the lilac bushes outside the "Old House." I can best remember that deep droning as it passed through the quiet night just south of Grandpa's farm. If parents have you witness such memorable historic sights so that you will always remember them, mine succeeded.

The doves are cooing in my backyard. They are not at all peaceful. Maybe it's because they're not pure white? With sharp beaks, they peck at the little birds trying to feed with them under the lighthouse feeder that Lisa gave me. Birds have always been a part of our lives here: whip-poor-wills, owls (Uncle Nard and cousin Ralph Hawkins shot a great grey owl out in the pine barrens, south of Wildfields. It was stuffed and mounted on the living room wall for all the years that I lived at Wildfields). Eventually it was invaded by mites and is gone, who knows where.

After we moved to Wildfields, swifts circled their living quarters in the big chimney of the "Old House." Once Aunt Margaret kept a canary in the sunporch where it was warm. Its morning singing made us all happy. Two Canada geese flew from the pond every early morning out over the small area left of the pine barrens – I hear them everyday just at dawn or soon after.

One day feathered creatures left an indelible imprint on my brain. Carol came to visit with her then three little children. It was summer and we headed out toward the bay to feed the swans. We stopped where the stone wall runs along Shore Road and got out with our giant bag of popcorn. Mother Swan, several babies and Papa Swan were swimming close to shore. The children threw popcorn into the marsh between them and the water. Father Swan was interested and waddled out toward us but we couldn't get the popcorn far enough to attract Mama and her babies.

"Here," said know-it-all Grandma. "Give me the bag and I'll go out toward them." I dropped down from the stone wall and gingerly walked through the wet marsh toward the babies and began throwing handfuls of popcorn. Pop Swan was now very definitely interested in the popcorn I thought!

He came waddling toward me swaying his huge body back and forth. Now he was behind me and I turned to feed him. But it wasn't concern for popcorn that brought him. It was concern for his babies.

Out went his great wings and his huge neck and sharp beak were swinging back and forth as he let out shrill, hissing cries. "Get away," he was screaming and became even more menacing. I turned away and ran as fast as the wet grass would allow, Father Swan chasing me, popcorn flying and Lisa, Marc, Michele and Carol all laughing hysterically.

It's spring again and if Grandpa and Uncle Nard were here, they would be out burning all the lawns – pails of water nearby and wet brooms in their hands to beat out the flames if they got too lively. You could burn leaves in the autumn, too. The smell of bonfires was everywhere.

So many rules and regulations have come since suburbia ringed Wildfields: no burning, no fireworks, proof of residency to use West Meadows Beach or to park on the docks, no burial of pets on your property, no hunting, and on and on.

Where only the tiny mail plane flew overhead, now giant jets go into Islip at MacArthur Airport, helicopters race to the landing pad at Stony Brook University Hospital. On Leonard's birthday in 1996, two hundred and thirty people died when TWA flight 800 crashed into the Atlantic Ocean just a few miles off the coast of East Moriches. Friends died in World War II, Vietnam and Korea. The world was opened up to us through television – John and Mary Hawkins and Soreno Burnell only knew the way across the ocean from England. Vic and Bart and Russell fought in strange tropical lands never heard of by Simeon and Merritt. Nelson landed fighter planes on carriers that could have easily held all the ships that brought our ancestors to this country.

Other things never change – especially our love and needs for each other.

The little red barn stands as it always did at the edge of the field south of Wildfields. Something, probably raccoons, has put a large hole in the eastern door that opened into the cow stalls. Grandpa would milk the cows – or later the one cow, "Pet" – and then take them out through that door and tether them in the field. The cows would eat a circle around the stake by the time they were brought in for evening milking. Once Al Hobbs brought a mule there to pull his plow. He'd have to push the mule's rump to get him going, he was so stubborn. I often tried to pull him ahead by his rope but it never worked for me. "Stubborn as a jackass." For sure!

Mr. Hobbs used an old fashioned hand-pushed cultivator to keep those fields weed-free for years when he planted crops here. Eventually he bought a tractor. Occasionally his wife would help with the crops and she'd squat in the field picking beans with a crew of three or four helpers and her Mason jar of whiskey.

Like the rest of us, the barn stands lonely now. The students' cars are parked all over the south lawn at Wildfields. We walk over and count them daily and when none but Dave's are left, Len "house sits." We used to play marbles out there. Merle was so good that Muriel and I soon kept our favorites inside the house because we knew that Merle would win them. She had a huge cloth bag of them pulled tight with a drawstring. We'd scratch a big two-foot circle in the sand with a stick and the fun began. And everyday she'd wipe us out and we'd have to use part of our allowance to buy more. We also all had kazoos, a small instrument that you put into your mouth and hummed a song. Our "kazoo band" drove the family crazy with the raspy tones. Merle also played her Jew's harp: another metal instrument that you held in your mouth and twanged a steel string – opening and closing your mouth to raise and lower the notes. We also all had harmonicas, even graduating to ones that had a side button that you pushed to change the key. Muriel bought a guitar when in high school and took lessons for a short time. One Christmas Mom and Dad gave me a xylophone, which I still have. It was made of wood and was owned by a friend of Dad's who played it in a band. One spring, the music teacher, Mrs. Boomer, convinced me to play in the band since she had no one to play the glockenspiel. I thought it was wonderful. We never could join the band because rehearsals were after school and we had no way to get home. Not that I didn't walk home occasionally, in fact I did so quite often during soccer season when I played on the team. From the hill above where Mario's restaurant now is to Wildfields was often a long, lonely cold walk – but only for the one season. Band or orchestra went on all year long. When Carol was a baby, and Nelson and I were living at Wildfields, I walked her in her carriage one day over to Mary Reboli's and back when she lived in Stony Brook. Now I find it hard to walk around the block! Sometimes we walked home from work at the Stony Brook School in the summers. I started there when I was fifteen. Muriel and I climbed the water tower there more than once. The open ladder went up to the bottom of the tower filled with water and then jutted outward, backwards, around the railing of the walkway that surrounded the tank. Once over that fearful spot, the view was spectacular!

How quickly the nest at Wildfields emptied. Merle went to St. John's Hospital in Brooklyn, New York, from which she graduated as a registered nurse; Muriel went to New Paltz State Teachers College and then to New York Dietetic Institute from which she graduated as a dietitian; and I went to New Paltz State Teachers College from which I graduated as a licensed New York State teacher. My first job was as a fifth-grade teacher in the Roeliff-Jansen Central School at Hillsdale, New York. Among the students in my first class was the Methodist minister's son, a lovely boy and great student that I adored. My first obvious sin was the Halloween Party that I gave the class in October. One parent offered to sell me apple cider at .25 cents a gallon for the event and I took him up on it immediately. I bought boxes of large doughnuts and made popcorn the night before. The party was held, as all school class parties are, at the last hour of the school day. I lined up the four gallon jugs of cider on the table by my desk, had one student pass out napkins and paper plates, went around spooning out popcorn and delivering doughnuts to each, and then poured out paper cups of cider. Never having had a class party before, I was amazed at the mounting crescendo as the kids enjoyed themselves. It became louder and louder and they became wilder and wilder. Then popcorn began to fly. I didn't think I liked any of this party idea, but since every other class was having one, I knew it had to take place. I was so relieved when the busses took them all away!

An hour later I had finally cleared up the mess in my room. I couldn't believe all the cider they had drunk and how they kept coming for more. I was so busy pouring and scolding popcorn throwers, that I couldn't think. There was one partial gallon of cider left so I took it home to the boarding house where about five of us lived and we relaxed before dinner. It didn't take long to discover the cider was hard! In my first two months of teaching, I sent the minister's son home drunk! Off to a great start!

After World War II ended, I taught first and second grade at Port Jefferson Station Comsewogue School. I also taught at many other schools: third and fourth grade at the little old Stony Brook Elementary School (long gone); first and third grade at a school in West Babylon; first grade in Miami,

Florida; second grade and then later first grade in Trenton; New Paltz (where all my training was in seventh, eight and ninth grades); Bedford Hills (where it was in fourth, fifth, sixth and third); Middletown, New York where I taught third and later first grade; and Port Jefferson Station where I taught second and later first.

For forty years of my life, I spent most of my days with children. I'll never regret that. It's just amazing what *they* taught *me*!

I'm pretty sure that Mom told me that Sarah Ann once taught in the little schoolhouse at the foot of the hill. Perhaps this was before she married Ebenezer Hawkins – the one who committed suicide in the "Old House" after her death. (There was another Ebenezer Hawkins who committed suicide or was murdered in the woods south of here. Grandpa found the body with his throat slit. I personally doubt that Ebenezer did that to himself! But what a traumatic find.)

David fills me in with these stories. As I've said, I could not have written this without his never-ending help.

Here is some more history I recently gleaned from him:

William Hawkins had nine children. The eldest child was Anna who died young while her children, and Merritt's, were very young. She was the first bride to live in the "Old House." She was born in 1782 and married Merritt. Their youngest child, Decatur, was only two when his mother died.

Another son of William's was Elkanah who was a blacksmith in Stony Brook. His daughter, Amanda Maria, married Louis Selleck of Middletown, New York. William's daughter, Ruth, was eighteen years younger than Anna. When she was four years old, her father died and she came to live with her sister Anna in the "Old House." Anna raised this little sister and she in turn probably helped raise Anna's daughter, Sarah Ann, when she was old enough to help. Ruth married Nichol Smith. Their first child, Daniel, was probably named for his uncle, who had married two of Simeon's daughters (at different times in his life of course!) These girls were twins and neither had any children by Daniel. Ruth's grave is in the southeast corner of our Methodist churchyard in Setauket. *(Personal note to Linda Baldo: She's your great – seven times – Aunt Ruth. Should you decide to look for the grave!)*

David Selleck has written out the progression of the land here at Wildfields up through the time of Simeon Hawkins' living there (in what later became the "Carriage House"). I've enclosed it just as David wrote it.

Note: Joseph Ackerly's Path is now Pond Path; Nassakeag swamp is now our little pond below the "Old House." Some of Simeon's orchard can still be found on the Nassakeag school grounds; the Widow Bigg's lot is where the "Old House" now stands. South line is uncertain, but probably ended at Tom Hawkins pond (Hub Road).

David's notes read:

Late 1600's – town lays out 100 acres at Nassakeag to George Phillips, Pastor of Setauket Presbyterian Church.

May 1713 – Reverend George Phillips gives deed to the 100 acres to Eleazer Hawkins (born 1688) who was about age 25 at the time.

Most likely Reverend Phillips 100 acres was deeded to Eleazer's son, Alexander, at some point, although the deed may have been lost. Alexander was coincidently born in 1713, the same year his father bought the 100 acres. Various fragments of memory over the years tell me (David B. Selleck) that the settlement up at Hub Road, which was probably founded by Alexander Hawkins, was started in the 1730's or early 1740's. This settlement included the southeast part of the 100 acres. Alexander would have been about twenty-seven years old in 1740.

At some point in the 18th Century, Reverend Phillips 100 acres was partitioned. In the last half of the eighteenth century. Alexandra's son, Simeon, received a deed for a section of the 100 acres.

Grandpa owned over 300 acres, including land at West Meadow and Centereach. He played the stock market without fear in the 1920's. He had never had a failure there – until the Wall Street market crash of 1929. He had gotten rid of surplus acreage before that; probably to invest since he had great luck with his first stocks.

Grandpa once took me to the locations of the West Meadows property and the New Village farm. He told David that he remembered going there as a boy with his father, Ethelbert, to get cordwood to put on a sloop sailing from Stony Brook to New York City.

Floyd Holgerson (Hattie's husband, Alice's dad) remembered Ethelbert Sr. staying at Holgerson's after the death of his wife, Hester Ann, in 1905. He had a room there and also ate there, napping on the living room couch. He would take his scythe and cut the grass along the roadside. Kenny Tuck lives in that house now. The original home burned and the one now standing there was built on the cellar of the "Old House" about 100 years ago. It desperately needs repairs, but Kenny is ill and has very little money.

Grandpa's subdued personality ever comes to me in bits and pieces as I write this. Mom told me of the time he was teaching her to drive his new car. They were in Port Jefferson and in those days one could make a U-turn on East Main Street near the Baptist church (as _we_ often did up until recently. Mom was making this U-turn when she lost control of the car which then jumped the curb and landed in the window of Dare's Drug Store. Grandpa's single and only comment: "Lordy, Lordy." The weekly newspaper read: **Gas Buggy Calls on Druggist.**

Mom always had difficulty driving. She looked through the steering wheel of her Oldsmobile, not over it. Steering wheels were open and not obstructed by dashboards then. Sitting on her car cushion she could barely reach the pedals.

Her great-grandson, Marc Bonney, now drives 18-wheelers across the United States. Wonder what Mom would think of that?

Leonard goes over to Wildfields every weekday that David isn't out, when none of the Chinese students are there. I'd be remiss if I didn't included Len's favorite tale:

Cousin Edith and Cousin Charles lived with Aunt Aurelia Gray (Edith's mother) in her home on Route 25A in Setauket. Her sister, Oneres, lived in Morristown, New Jersey as did her son, Orville Ackerly Hawkins, born in 1889. Edith and Orville were first cousins, but this didn't stop Orville from becoming infatuated with Edith – married or not. Orville decided to act on his infatuation and one day (or night) he hid in the bushes along 25A in front of Aunt Aurelia's home. Cousin Charles came out to his car parked in the front and Orville shot him. The bullet lodged so close to Charlie's heart that it couldn't be removed. He lived with if for years until his eventual death. Orville was arrested and faced life in prison. On his way to Riverhead jail, the sheriff gave him permission to say good-bye to his family on Long Island. They arrived at Wildfields and Mom and Nana hid Cousin Edith and Cousin

Charles in the attic. We three girls were put in the upstairs bathroom and told to lock the door. Orville knew that Edith was there because he saw her car. Finally, the sheriff led him away and we all came out of hiding. We were five, seven and eight respectively, and it left quite an impression on all three of us. Orville then went with the sheriff to see his brother, Ralph Hawkins, in East Setauket (Amy Huskisson was Ralph's daughter and Sandy Loudicina his great-granddaughter). He went in to say good-bye, took an overdose of pills and died on their kitchen floor. The name Orville stands for the "O" in O.B. Davis funeral parlors (Orville Burnell Davis – all relatives!) located in Port Jefferson, Miller Place and Centereach.

Life rolls along. You recall things in bits and pieces, things that happened to you; things that you were told.

Life wasn't always sad, but sometimes it surely was. Life wasn't always funny, but sometimes it surely was. Sometimes it was "God awful," like when Nana or Mom put drops of kerosene in a spoonful of sugar and made us swallow it to cure our croup. Sometimes it was hard – hard for the farmers and builders and weavers of flax and wool to make linsey-woolsey blankets and shirts – hard for the sick and dying and those left behind.

But surely we all shed tears for the pain of each new generation.

Early morning sunlight sifts through the huge maple trees in my backyard. I'm trying to beat the ninety-plus heat forecast for today. Yesterday it hit ninety-four degrees with high humidity. I'm having a new roof put on at 8 Storybook Lane and the roofer also arrived before 7a.m. trying to beat the heat, too.

Puffs of steam came from the iron. When we were kids, the iron was a triangular piece of iron with a handle that was heated by putting it on the coal stove top. Fires burned in these stoves all summer since they were also the only source of heat for cooking. Later, when we moved to Wildfields and had electricity, we had electric irons, but no steam irons. They are the most recent development and now almost everyone owns one. The old irons were kept in shape by running beeswax wrapped in cloth back and forth across the bottom. Now a damp rag keeps new irons clean – and better yet, most materials don't need to be ironed!

Leonard, who sees his psychiatrist on a monthly basis now for medication and treatment of his bi-polar clinical depression, told me of his last visit. The doctor is very friendly and they discuss all sorts of things apparently. He asked Len what he was reading. With great glee he told him "Benjamin Franklin's 'Fart Proudly'"— which he was indeed reading. I'm sure that was well-planned! Thank God for laughter. And thank God for the availability of the University Hospital and Medical Center. He has had great doctors and stabilization, thanks to them.

The buildings of the Medical Center at S.U.N.Y (State University of New York)Stony Brook loom on the horizon near our home and Wildfields. In the winter with the tree leaves gone, you can see the lights in rooms in Suffolk's only "sky-scrapers," the University hospital and the Medical Center buildings both within walking distance of my home. Doctors Sereno Burnell, Junior and Senior, would have been lost in the maze of the hospital and never found their way home to Wading River or Miller Place – or even Main Street Setauket! They totally missed laser surgery, radiation, nuclear medicine, antibiotics, vitamins, birth control pills, chemotherapy, cataract removal, mastectomies, disc surgery, polio vaccines and probably thousands of other medical practices and procedures widely used today. And there surely would have been no room to park their horses and buggies!

From Sereno Burnell to today has been a long space of time, but Merle was a nurse; Cousin Edith a licensed practical nurse; Linda is a nurse; Vic's grandfather was a doctor – a "country doctor" like Sereno. Dr. Seitz, David's youngest son and his son's wife – William and Meredith Selleck – are both doctors; and Vic's daughter Susy is a lab technician. Muriel was a hospital dietitian.

Teachers abound also in the family. According to Mom, either Sarah Ann or her daughter taught at the little schoolhouse at the foot of Pond Path. (It is now in the Museums of Stony Brook complex). Aunt Margaret taught business subjects in Port Jefferson High School and in West Babylon. Vic's brother Leonard was a teacher in Ambridge, Pennsylvania. Vic was a coach, physical education teacher and science teacher in Pennsylvania; West Babylon, New York; Trenton, Florida; and Middletown, New York. David Selleck taught in the science department at New Rochelle, New York. Burnell Selleck teaches at Michigan State in its medical and science departments; Della Baldo taught reading and worked in the guidance department. George Baldo, her son who married Merle's daughter, teaches at SUNY at Stony Brook in the medical research department. And me, again, I spent forty years teaching in elementary schools.

We weren't / aren't famous, but we contributed. There were few famous people living out here when we were kids. Now, now they are a dime a dozen.

Charles Ruggles sat across from us in the Presbyterian Church when he was here in the summer. Newspaper columnist and film actor Robert Benchley visited. Our high school English teacher, Margaret Skinner, was the niece of author/actress Cornelia Otis Skinner. And Hans von Kaltenborn, world-famous radio commentator, built his home, Point-of-View, overlooking West Meadows Creek on Mount Gray Road.

The last two generations have attended college, and mine was the very first to leave Wildfields and become educated. Leonard and George graduated from SUNY Stony Brook – on land adjoining Grandpa's. Leonard walked to classes on paths where Dad and Grandpa walked to the train station; George received his doctor's degree from Stony Brook and teaches and conducts research there as well. Leonard still connects with professors, now friends, and is on the President's Advisory Committee for the Disabled on campus. I often sit and wait for him and watch the students. They are so young. They aren't afraid. There is no war going on which might snatch them away. They have money for cars. Few have to work their way through. Their clothes are crazy looking, but the long hair is gone. They're just students.

The sweet aroma of toasted potato bread greeted me as I came in the back door after having gone next door to Alexander's to feed Figaro, their cat. All is quiet at Wildfields. It's early Saturday morning and the beginning of Memorial Day weekend. Not much is moving out there yet. The rising sun hits the huge white azalea in the front yard as I go to the front door and step out on the porch. I collect the empty dishes where Leonard has fed the stray neighborhood cats in the night. I recognize the woman coming down the street with her dog and we call a mutual friendly "Hello."

I think about Michele and all her ugly problems with Lee Cohen whom she married less than a year ago. She had been here with her daughter Maddy last week to begin scraping and painting this house to get money to move away from him. She'd be here today but he told Lisa (while Michele was working) that she would not sleep in "his" house one more night, so she's looking for a place to stay. She's with Lisa now and I'm sure that's a difficult situation, space-wise. How cruel mankind is.

On the lighter side, Dave Selleck was out this week and we drove over to Port Jefferson, to Cedar Hill Cemetery where Vic is buried. I had not been back there in at least ten years – I'm not a cemetery person, not for returning to those recently departed at least. I loved them as they walked the earth and through my life. Now it's just a stone, a piece of recorded history.

Anyhow, we arrived just after the cemetery gates opened at 8:30 a.m. I knew the route to the top of the hill where I'd parked before. After we got out to walk to the area where I thought Vic was buried, I got lost. A great expanse of land had been cleared, edged by rows of recent 1990's graves. His had been at the edge of the woods. We walked every roadway, circling the entire cemetery. We found Nicky Poulos' grave, the Holgersen's, and countless of other recognizable names. Two hours later we had not found Vic's resting place. "I figure he's mad at me for not coming sooner," I said to David, "and he's left." We laughed and headed for where we could see Dave's car on the little hill. There was one more road off to the opposite side from where I believed Vic's stone to be. On one side were graves in a row covered with toys and flowers, obviously children. We went a little further and there on the hillside next to the woods was ROTHERMEL as big and clear as day. It had taken me two hours to find my husband's grave! That seems to say something, but I'm not sure what! I'm still laughing about it and I've promised to take Leonard up there soon before I forget the way again.

When I told Carol this story today, she laughed and then remarked, "How strange. I never dream about Dad, but the day after you were up there, I had an unpleasant dream about him."

I guess he really was mad!

This Memorial Day weekend I hung the flag outside in his honor and for all who fought in our wars. I often think: Why did they fight? Perhaps because they wanted to, perhaps because we made them. Setauket will hold its annual parade down Main Street from the Village Green by the Presbyterian Church to the small park at the foot of the hill. There the plaque is embedded in stone telling of all the friends I knew that died in a war that covered two parts of this planet. But who wants to go to a parade alone?

When we were children we honored the dead on Decoration Day which was always May 30th. Grandpa filled a large container with water. We three girls helped Mom pick lily of the valley, iris and violets, and Nana made bouquets tied with string around wet cloth at their base. She stayed at home while Grandpa and Mom drove us to Mount Sinai to the grave sites of Sereno and Ruth Burnell, and others I've long since forgotten in that family and Aunt Ardie's nearby. We poured water into mason jars from the big container and arranged the bouquets at the front of each stone. Grandpa would nod his head as each bouquet was completed, smoke trailing from his pipe and a contented, "Hmmm..." from his lips. Then back to Port Jefferson in time for the parade.

It was years before I ever went to a grave site with anything but the feeling of joy of a holiday sort. Not until the loss was closely mine.

My flag snaps in this morning's breeze saluting Bart, Russell and Victor who all left our shores to fight in World War II. Somewhere along his journey from Camp Lejeune, North Carolina to California to the Philippines,

Guam and Iwo Jima, Vic met screen actor Tyrone Power who was in his division. Once he was sent up with a message and, I think, his paycheck to rouse the sleeping Tyrone and give it to him. *What did he look like?*, I wonder. A movie star as handsome as Tyrone Power was curled up in a bunk in some far -place. *Was his hair rumpled? Did he look like the thousands of other marines in their skivvies? Did he give a damn who saw him? Or did he just not want to die?*

The war brought many technological changes. Aircraft were revolutionized and they became faster and more maneuverable. The world was suddenly closer. Cars had automatic shifts instead of manual clutches. Previously, in order to signal turning, we had to manually lower the driver's side window, push our arms out with hand pointing left for the left turn; hand bent backward and pointing right for a right turn. Not only was it awkward, it was cold in winter and very wet in rain. Now turn signals are used.

The banditos are back. That's the name that Leonard and Carol's three kids gave to the family of five raccoons that were here all one summer. We saw Papa Raccoon occasionally, but Mama and her three babies came by in broad daylight. Michele, Marc and Lisa fed them pieces of bread with peanut butter and honey. Raccoons are said to probably be ill if they come out in daylight, but these seemed perfectly healthy. Marc just sent me a card with three raccoons on it when he and Ellen were traveling in his huge truck. The baby banditos grew of course, and then we saw them at night. Sometimes they got in our garage and somehow, someone, not from our house, put cowbells on their necks! One night we heard them racing around our attic above the den. We'd boarded up the opening many times, but cats and squirrels – and God knows what else – still find a way into the attic. Last night Leonard saw another group of small banditos with parents. Their habitat is disappearing fast. David's and Burnell's woods are soon going to be all that is left of it on Pond Path where once they had miles of roaming space, as did the fox and opossum and turtles. There was never a spring when someone didn't bring a box turtle in to school.

David Selleck came in today and we sat talking over coffee. He had a marvelous book with him, The Records of the Town of Brookhaven up to 1800, compiled by the town clerk. It outlines meetings held from the time of Indian deeds to acres of land, beaches, rights with their "X" mark next to their native names up to a survey of lands in 1797. The excerpts are fascinating. One reads: 2007 "At a meeting of ye Trustees, on the Second Day of June present: Mr. Woodhull, Samuel Tomson, Andrew Miller and John Wood ordered that from this time forward, that, if any of ye Trustees doth not appear at ye time, and place, shall forfeit a pint of Rum."

David believes that this book, which belonged to Ethelbert Selleck, was one he obtained after moving from Middletown, New York to Long Island to try and trace his wife's (Hester Ann) roots and how the land was acquired.

From records of Town of Brookhaven meetings, in a lawsuit from 1666, it reads: "Zackary Hawkins, plaintive, Robert Ackerly, defendant, in a action of trespass, for his hoggs destroying my peas, to the value of eight bushels of peas, for which the plantive desires the judgement of the court.

The judgement of the court is, that we fine for the plantive four bushels of peas."

(Better luck than I had collecting from Nelson Ackerly!)

The land that was called Phillips 100 acres, and eventually held Simeon Hawkins' home, was, according to the records of the Town of Brookhaven on "Nov. ye 12th, 1697 required as follows: "Laid out for Mr. George Phillips 100 acres of Land, which the Town gave him. Living near Nassakeag Swamp, butting and bounding as follows: on ye north side of the Land beginning at a white oake. Tree marked four sides. Running Westerly to the middle of saide Nassakeag Swamp, joyning to the land of John Biggs and from thence

Running a little Southerly to another white oake tree marked four sides, and from thence Southerly to a red oake under a hill marked four sides, running Easterly by the said hill to a chestnut tree marked four sides to ye Easterward of a Round Swamp, so returning northerly to the first Whiteoak Tree where first began by me."

Richard Woodhull,
Surveyor.

David fills me in on so many parts of my history. He is so intelligent, so knowledgeable.

In the records of Brookhaven (Town of) for 1679-1756 he shows me where "John Biggs is granted five acres at the western swamp (our pond)." Water rights were later bought by our family. This is probably the widow Bigg's lot. Thomas Biggs Sr. had several children. Mary who married Zackary Hawkins and whose son Eleazer was born in 1688 and who bought the 100 acres from Phillips and John, Eleazer's uncle, who received the Nassakeag lot in 1684. (This is what Dave believes is so, but is still looking for concrete proof. John may or may not have built a home there, perhaps just a barn for sheep. There is a well below the "Old House" other than the one on the path to the pond, making one suspect there was a building there before Merritt built in 1802.

Our memories shake and rattle and pieces fly off into today. The seasons change and new things surface from some hiding places never known. I remember Dad, Uncle Nard and Grandpa all put away their soft, gray fedora hats in June and out came the stiff, off-white straw panama hats. The brims were circled with dark ribbons and I wondered how they kept these hard things on their heads. The women followed suit with their soft felt and dark straws for the white and flowered straws with flimsy veils. Their dark gloves changed to white with tiny pearl buttons at their wrists. That would not be me today! I'd leave a glove in every restaurant and I hate hats! Of course we never ate in a restaurant until we were grownups. All the *changing* took place at the end of June and on Labor Day. God forbid you wore white after that! Children's Day at church was in June and we all had new white dresses for that event, and black patent leather shoes – of course.

Mom, who was 4 feet 11 inches tall, wore a size four shoe. Often the shoe stores didn't have her size. Sometimes they sold her the display shoes which were that small. I can even recall her buying children's shoes for herself.

It's morning, and its freshness is everywhere. A soft rain fell throughout the night. Gracie is up on the roof, "meowing" for me to get her down. It's her little game. If I play and start around the side of the house calling her, she will have jumped into the Quanson cherry tree before I even get there. I swear she's even smiling as she climbs down the trunk to the fork where I can reach to pet her. "Gotcha, Mom." She bounds across the yard in front of me, behind me: up a tree trunk, down a tree trunk, bouncing and hopping, more like a rabbit than a cat. Outside, the smell of fresh paint permeates the air. My granddaughter, Michele, a single mother of a two-year-old girl, has put a primer coat on the front of the house. She worked all weekend and it looks great. *Who says young people are spoiled and lazy?* She rummages through the old photos stretched across the dining room table. "Maddy looks like Mom." She does not see my face as the Burnells and Hawkins of long ago. This, too, is part of our heritage.

Muriel and I never like Florida as a place for a permanent home. Merle loved it. The hotter it got, the better it was for her. In 1959 Vic and I found teaching jobs in Middletown, New York, and happily returned north. Two years later, Russ asked for a transfer and he and his family moved to Mechanicsburg, Pennsylvania – where they rented a one-story house. Russ decided that he needed more bedroom space for his three children and so, without asking his landlord's permission, he raised the roof of the house high enough to make two more bedrooms in the new second story. Russ did this whole procedure without help, using his car to pull the roof up. Unbelievable! A year later, he bought a home in Camp Hill, Pennsylvania, where they lived until after Muriel's death. Within two more years, Merle and her family were all back on Long Island. Not out of choice, though. She was dying, and wanted to be near family. Sometimes our choices in life are made for us.

The "tribe" has scattered. Mickey remains in Florida, Kevin in the west which his Grandfather John loved; Carol in Missouri near where Aunt Una (Burnell) Norris once lived; Burnell in Michigan where his mom's family lives; Margaret in Baltimore, Maryland near her dad who lives with his friend Betty in Hershey, Pennsylvania; Frank (Jay) in New Jersey; Kathy in Fort Lee, New Jersey; and Linda and I are still on what was Grandpa's land. David lives in Pelham, New York and would be here if he could.

They have no way of knowing that they are cutting into our memories, chopping them into tiny pieces in their shredder. The family next door is having old trees removed and shredded. This is the apple tree at the end of the lawn, just east of the path that we made carting tin cans to the pile beyond the hedge. The machine groans and wails and screams as the arms of trees that held us are ground to dust. Trees have marked boundaries, held bird nests and squirrel homes, given fruit for pies and canning. Muriel's son Kevin was here from Colorado this summer and couldn't wait to have his young son, Cameron, climb the maple at Wildfields that he once climbed as a little boy.

There are very few oak trees at Wildfields, except down by the pond. I always wanted one somewhere in my yard but never could get a seedling to survive. When Muriel died, one started growing just west of my backyard patio. It now towers above the house. "My Muriel Tree."

Years ago we visited Aunt Una and Uncle Ray in their Cedar Grove home. They had an extensive backyard. Uncle Ray Norris had a great sense of humor. Two fairly small beech trees grew at the far end. "One is a beech, the other a son-of-a beech," he laughingly told us.

Our ancestors came to America to make a better life for themselves. I hope they did. I'm sure that they struggled through some very difficult times. But then, haven't we all?

Merle, Muriel, David, Burnell and I grew up in a bigoted WASP Community. I can't speak for David and Burnell because I wasn't close to them as they grew into the age where you make decisions regarding your beliefs. I do know that Merle and Muriel carried many of those beliefs with them. Merle literally believed that blacks belonged in the back of the bus; Muriel hated the blacks – some blacks – for moving into and "spoiling" her community. Was it the black's who spoiled it – or the whites contention that they were less of a group of people than they were? My closeness to Dad definitely had an affect on me. He saw blacks, Indians, Jews, Chinese, whites, as all the same and taught me to believe that. What a wonderful life it has given me: friends of all nationalities, colors, and beliefs. Dad was right.

When we graduated from grade school and high school we were presented with bouquets and baskets of flowers by our families at the end of the ceremony. Some kids had seven or eight, some had one. The kids from Chicken Hill didn't have any. Dad thought that whole scene was wrong.
We never invited our black friends or Polish or Jewish friends to our parties. The kids from Chicken Hill never had any parties.

We came here generations ago but we are no better – no worse – than anyone who just became a citizen today. It's fun to trace our ancestry back, to see and know where we came from, how and why. But don't ever let it give you the imprint of snobbery that our families knew. God gave us all everything that we have – we are – we gave to our children. And he loves us all the same. That knowledge is what I leave you. I have a feeling that most of you already know that.

Today I look past the clotheslines, past Wildfields, past the "Old House" and write of the songs in my heart. There is still such peace here as the shadows fall and lights go on – and the ghosts of the past whisper to me from the fields.

"Shalom," Wildfields. Keep singing.

Merritt Hawkins Home in 1996 Pond Path in foreground

Merritt Hawkins house in background; Wild fields in center. Picture taken from path leading from 8 Storybook Lane and our backyard.

Merritt Hawkins Homestead b. 1802

1921

Windows on bottom left are in living room. Bottom right was our bedroom. House faces south on Pond Path.

Kitchen extension was added (shown right) and later removed by Margaret Selleck. Pump house shown at right in front of kitchen door has also been removed as "city water" came through.

When Ardelle and Bernard moved in they used the bedroom above us.

This picture, taken in 1934, shows little change. Kitchen is still on North side. Snow was melting following a blizzard.

The Carriage House on the west side of Pond Path. Today, the Nassakeag School would lie in the background. This was once the home of Simeon Hawkins. The window (top left) was in the little room where Dad and I spent many hours. The door on left goes into the room where sleighs were kept.

The old sheep-barn is at the far left.

1924 - a car sends up a cloud of dust next to the Carriage House on Pond Path

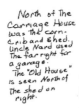

North of The Carriage House was the corn-crib and shed. Uncle Nard used the far right for a garage. The "Old House" is seen North of the shed on right.

Dad watches Pet with her calf.

Uncle Nard and Aunt Ardie start on a ride with Shea. They are at the intersection of Upper Sheep Pasture Rd. and Pond Path. The field behind is just north of where Wildfields stands today.

Dad, John Pettit, stands in what is now the front lawn of Wildfields. Merritt Hawkins Homestead is in background.

South of the field above were the old barns; on the left, the horse barn and the long low cow barn behind.
Merle is in the center and the women are probably her grandmother Whittesey (left) and Aunt Leslie (right.)

1920 Elsie Burnell Selleck

Ethelbert H. Selleck when he first came to Setauket

– and at age 70 in 1938 – he was still the "gentleman farmer."

Ruth (left) and Muriel (right) with their dolls and rockers Summer 1927 and with Mom in 192

Carleton Norris (Eunice Burnell Norris son)
Ruth, Muriel, Merle   Sept. 1927

Muriel holding her red elephant

4 yrs   almost 6   7

1925

Ruth (left) and Muriel Pettit at "Old House"
    Pond Path, Setauket, NY

2 yr.   3½ yr.

Muriel, Merle and Ruth by horse barn

3½   5 yr.   2 yr.

Muriel and Ruth

In 1928 we moved to Wildfields.

L to R. Ruth, Merle, Muriel on Children's Day in June in our "Sunday Best."

The house nears completion.

Winter of 1928. We three girls with a long-time family friend, Roxie Davenp and our two pets — Rex, the collie, and Don, the mutt.

Muriel, Merle, Ruth

Trevorton, Pa.
1977
Leonard H. Rothermel
Leonard J. Rothermel
Victor O. Rothermel

1978

Uncle Leonard, Len.
Aunt May O'Rourke
(Vic's brother and sister.)

Leonard J., Leonard H., May

1989

Len has done volunteer work for the handicapped for years. He has been on the Presidents Advisory Board for the Disabled for over 25 years.

In 1995, he was honored for this achievement. Here he is with me and with Dr. Richard Solo who was also awarded.

Printed in the United States
115470LV00006B/1-99/P